GERARD GORMAN was born and reared in Newcastle, County Down, and now lives in Poyntzpass. He has spent most of his working life as a painter and decorator.

DAMIAN GORMAN is a poet and playwright. His selected poems and memoir, *As If I Cared*, is also available from Blackstaff Press.

'Gerard Gorman's courageous testimony must be heeded. *So Young* is a damning indictment of Catholic Church policy which hid criminals from the law. There is a clue in the subtitle of the book, for it is indeed living proof of how a powerful religious organisation allowed innocent young children to have their lives taken. *So Young* is heartbreaking at times, yet uplifting at other moments, as Gerard tries to live normally, but all the while dealing with everyday events that trigger flashbacks to the horrors of his childhood. He hides all from his loved ones and keeps his suffering secret. *So Young* is a harrowing but compelling read, and this heroic story will undoubtedly inspire others to come forward and find voice.'

CHRIS MOORE, the award-winning journalist who broke
the Fr Brendan Smyth child abuse scandal

'Of this I am sure – the full truth about the clerical abuse scandal in the Diocese of Dromore would never have been known were it not for Gerard Gorman's courage and determination over many years. Gerard has done a huge service not just to survivors of paedophile priest Fr Malachy Finegan, but to so many other victims and survivors of abuse to whom he has given voice, and who are finally getting the justice and support they need.'

CLAIRE McKEEGAN, solicitor and founding
partner, Phoenix Law

'What I love about this book is the intimate voice of the narrator, bearing witness to traumatic relational experiences in the family, boarding school and society of the times. His is a young and deeply moving voice. All of us who have survived traumatic experiences are invited to engage – to stand as fully as we can as ally to the suffering and beauty in the book.'

DR ROSIE BURROWS, relational resilience
psychotherapist and researcher

'A story of courage and tenacity, buried for so long in the mind of a boy who lived in two worlds, and one of those worlds just wouldn't let go. Trying to keep them separate wasn't soul-destroying, for the soul had already been destroyed at the hands of a paedophile priest, but it was silently consuming him. To try to be "normal" in a world that starts to spiral out of control – that in many cases chooses not to know or want to know – is the loneliest place of all. But he is not alone. For Gerard to break the silence and, in the brokenness, reach out to those closest to him – to be believed and really loved and supported – is what makes this book possible. And empowers him to reclaim (as he does) his twelve-year-old self.'

JON McCOURT, chair, Survivors North West

'"The buried thing in you doesn't stay buried forever ..." It emerges eventually through the determination of people like Gerard Gorman and his dear, dear family, his mother, his wife. This book is an inspiration for all who have suffered through the malign power of a corrupt institution.'

STEPHEN REA

SO YOUNG

GERARD GORMAN
with DAMIAN GORMAN

First published in 2022 by Blackstaff Press
an imprint of Colourpoint Creative Ltd
Colourpoint House
Jubilee Business Park
21 Jubilee Road
Newtownards BT23 4YH

Printed and bound by CPI Group UK Ltd, Croydon CRO 4YY

A CIP catalogue for this book is available from the British Library

ISBN 978-1-78073-341-8

www.blackstaffpress.com

For Deirdre, Ursula,
Gerard and Diarmaid,
and for the twelve-year-old me,
with love

Freedom is what you do
With what's been done to you.

John-Paul Sartre

CONTENTS

PART TWO

You may think you know something about people like me – people who have been abused in childhood – from the press and the media. But what you know is *about* it, round and about it, and what I want to do in this book is take you into the *heart* of it.

I want to keep you as close beside me on this journey as I possibly can.

PART ONE

Chapter 1

TULLYBRANNIGAN ROAD

I was born on 21 November 1958 in the beautiful resort town of Newcastle, County Down, in the north of Ireland. My father, Patrick, was a fishmonger, originally from Lisburn, County Antrim; and my mother, Marie (née Cull), was originally from Dromore, County Down. I was a healthy baby and there was much joy at my arrival. My mother had had a number of misses and my brother Patrick, who did come to term, had died shortly after his birth. I was the first of my generation on the Cull side, and the first who would carry the Gorman name on the other.

When I was born, we lived in Slievecoole Park at the foot of the Mourne Mountains, and my first ever memory is of us moving to Tullybrannigan Road. I remember my first night there very clearly, although I couldn't have been much more than two and a half at the time. Mum was pregnant with my brother Damian, and for some reason she wasn't with Dad and me. I remember crying because she wasn't there, crying myself to sleep. She stayed up in Slievecoole Park that night, I don't know why. Maybe all the beds weren't made up yet;

maybe there'd been another row.

For some of the memories that have stayed with me from that early time are not so good. One day, for example, Damian and I were playing out in the back garden while Mum talked to a neighbour. Dad pulled into the drive, home from his fish shop, and was raising his voice even as he got out of the car. I don't know if it was a continuation of something from that morning or from a phone call, but he barely waited for the car to stop before he started. And it wasn't, 'Can you come into the house? I need to talk to you urgently.' Dad being Dad, it was just, *Bam!* Mum was shocked and crying, and I remember Dad being in her face, very threatening, until the neighbour's husband stepped out of their back door. I don't remember exactly what the man said, but it would have been something like, 'Calm down, Pat'. Dad said the equivalent of 'Well, you look after her,' and he lifted Mum over the wire fence that stood between the two houses and dropped her on to her knees on the other side.

Dad stormed into the house and the neighbours helped Mum to her feet. Me and my little brother Damian were in tears. I ran over to Mum, crying because she was crying. The couple took us into their kitchen and comforted us all.

Dad's was a small shop – The Bridge Fish Shop – in the centre of the town, near the river. It was beside The Bridge Butcher shop, and close to the amusement arcade and Mrs Boyle's chippy. Even in those early days I remember how calm it was when Dad was at work and it was just us and Mum.

Four children were born when we were in Tullybrannigan – Damian, Brendan, Declan and Moya: steps and stairs, a year between each. We never knew what sort of Dad was would come through the door, whether it would be Jekyll or Hyde. For he could be kind, 'out-of-character kind' nearly. Sometimes he would come home and kick ball with us for a bit while the tea was being made. There was another thing, a specific thing he did that stays with me. I remember him buying a Monkees LP for Declan, who was mad about them. He was very small, and hadn't asked for it, but Dad came home with the record for him one day, and it gave me a glow inside.

But often there was no involvement with him at all. Or worse.

One particular day, near teatime, Mum was ironing. When she'd finished, she put the ironing board away and went to the kitchen to put on the spuds. The iron was left sitting to cool. I flicked water at it while it was still hot, to make it hiss. This went down well with the wee ones, especially Declan who was the baby at the time. I remember the delight and the baby gurgles every time the iron started to *fizz*. But, unbeknown to me, Dad had come into the room and saw what I was doing. He absolutely blew his top. It was as if I had taken the baby's hand and placed it on the iron. And when the venom was at its height, Dad lifted the iron and put it on my left knee. I have the marks of it to this day. A huge blister came up on my knee, and I was drilled to tell the doctor 'exactly what had happened': that there'd been an accident in the kitchen, and I'd pulled boiling water from a pan down over myself. This was the same story I told the teachers in school.

I'd been afraid of Dad before, but that brought it to a different level.

Lifting his hand to us – and to Mum – was Dad's way of teaching lessons and settling arguments. It frightened me, and sometimes I needed a place to hide from him. I discovered, very young, a hiding place – a kind of tunnel – at the bottom of our back garden. It was between us and the boundary hedges of other gardens, some of which had differing lengths. If there was arguing, or Dad came home in a mood, I would go in there on my own, with a football. It was the first place that I'd created as a sanctuary for myself, this tunnel between hedges, but it wouldn't be the last.

I didn't live on my nerves every moment of my young life. I had friends, I was mad about football and I was reasonably happy at school, St Mary's Boys Primary, where I was quiet and very well-behaved – I didn't want any bad reports going home to my Dad. And I did like being a big brother to my four younger siblings; playing with them all in the back garden where Mum could keep an eye on us.

I also enjoyed visiting both sets of grandparents – staying over, being bathed in a tin bath and so on and, while I loved my Gorman grandparents (and was entranced by their cuckoo clock), there seemed to be more life and laughter with the Culls in Dromore. They were kind and sociable, and you never had to ask them for stuff. They had a bakery and shop, so things like confectionery and pastries were always to hand, or handed to you.

The beach was also important to me and I enjoyed

being near the sea and the sand. I wouldn't claim to have appreciated everything about it then, but Newcastle was a beautiful place to live and, looking back, I can see that I was witnessing the end of an era. There was a rag and bone man, Frank Connolly, who had a horse and cart, and a collie dog that would sit in the back. Frank did a bit of everything. If you were having renovations done, he'd go down to the block yard and get sand for you. I remember going out to the front garden just to see him going past. I wouldn't have done that for the sand lorry.

Frank lived in a wee cottage near the foot of the mountain – one of the last to go in the redevelopments. I could be wrong about this, but I think that Frank's own world changed after a big roll-over win at the parish bingo – a super prize of £500, which would have been a fortune then. He was probably retiring age anyway, but I don't remember hearing much *clippety-clop* after that.

The steep Tullybrannigan Road was a wee world of its own, particularly after Tullybrannigan Stores opened and you no longer had to go into the town itself for essentials. I remember the pride I felt when, in my early years at primary school, Mum gave me the list and money to go get a few items for the first time. But I remember, too, a bigger boy taking the money off me before I got to the shop one day. I ran home and told Mum what had happened. She kept faith with me and still sent me for messages, only now she had an arrangement with Oliver of Tullybrannigan Stores that I'd have a book with me, and he'd mark in the cost of what I got. There was no money involved now, but I was glad to be able to help Mum; glad that she didn't have to get everyone organised and out the door every time a message was needed.

But for all the responsibility, there was irresponsibility too. Once, when I was about seven or eight, I was kissed by an older woman! She was one year older than me and lived on the way to the shop. I had got a new bike, and she used to ask if she could have a go on it. I always said no, but one day she offered me a peck on the cheek in return. So I let her ride the bike to the corner. Good enough, she stopped at the corner, and waited for me to come and reclaim it.

And I loved when the circus came to town – the sheer glamour of the annual visit of Duffy's circus! I'd badger Mum to take me by the Donard Park, even before they were ready, just to see the stripes on the roof of the tent, or the horses outside. Because although we had the beach and the mountains – and that's what most people came to Newcastle for – to a wee boy like me this was what excitement was about: animals, clowns and acrobats. And Duffy's didn't come to every town, so it felt special. I really loved going – shouting when the clowns told us to shout; being amazed at the strongman and the acrobats. Though, young and all as I was, I did notice that the same person who'd been Bobo the clown from Czechoslovakia would later be introduced as a famous juggler from Poland or a Romanian knife-thrower. But it didn't matter. It was like something coming in from the outside world.

*

At this time, in the mid-sixties, I had my first taste (or tastes) of death. Mum's sisters, Kathleen and Agnes, had been visiting us one Sunday, along with Kathleen's husband, John, and our cousins, Patrick, Anne and baby Michael. That evening I knew something was badly wrong as a series of grim, hurried conversations took place above my head and Sarah Dornan – a friend of Mum's we called 'Aunt Sarah' – came over to mind us. Auntie Kathleen had been killed in a collision with another vehicle on the way home. Michael, who'd been sitting on her knee, died later from his injuries. Uncle John was in hospital for a very long time, blinded and hurt and Auntie Agnes, who was pregnant with her first child, lost the baby. Only Patrick and Anne, who were in the back seat, hadn't a scratch.

This was the first that I had ever really been around death. Auntie Kathleen and Michael had just been in our house, as large as life. *That can't be right, that they're dead*, I thought. *Sure they were only here. How can it be that suddenly they're not* anywhere *now?* It was followed, very quickly, by the death of Mum's father, Granda Cull. Everybody said that he'd died of a broken heart.

Yet, even though she'd lost her sister, her nephew and her Dad in such a short space of time, it was always Mum who came through in times like that; it was always her you could turn to. She got up in the morning, the housecoat went on, and that was her uniformed for work. And the work of her day – all her days – seemed to be loving us.

Chapter 2
MAIN STREET

The first time I heard we were moving from Tullybrannigan Road, Dad was still trading in The Bridge Fish Shop, and it was doing well. I was about nine or ten and my parents took me to this place further down Main Street where an old bicycle repair shop and a five-storey house were being refurbished by a firm called Bovaird and Ferguson and turned into a state-of-the-art fish shop, with floor-to-ceiling tiles and a walk-in cold room. There was a door from the back of the shop straight into the hallway of the house and, as we walked about I was told, 'This is your new home.'

The place had no garden, but if you went a few steps out the back of the house and along the alleyway past Dr Walsh's, you were on the beach. If you turned left, you were in the Downs Road Park, which was ideal for football. You could smell the sea from the back door. There was an excitement in that.

The reason for the move was to expand the business – the other shop was very small. And straight away the new place, The Sea Shell, went from being a fish shop to doing fresh fish, fruit and veg, and poultry, and in some ways what Dad did was ahead of its time. Nowadays the town is coming down with coffee houses and takeaways, but in those days, there were only a few cafes. What he did – and even the butchers weren't doing it then – was buy a barbecue machine and put it out on to the street. He would cook chicken and potted herrings to his own spice recipe. The smell of that wafting past, especially in the summer, encouraged families to buy whole chickens for their dinner – and he also did portions, served, like the whole birds, in tin foil bags. I remember, too, that he seemed to have asbestos hands. Where other staff needed knives and forks to portion the cooked chickens, he did it all by hand. The heat didn't bother him – 'Knives and forks be damned!'

People couldn't get enough of that chicken: bikers, people going on picnics or coming from the pub. Long before Kentucky Fried Chicken, there was my dad. And he was very busy. He opened seven days a week, and to 10 p.m. in the summer. Very quickly, he got a bigger machine – the biggest one available at the time. He was supplying the chippies in the town, the nursing homes and the Slieve Donard Hotel with fish. And often they decided they'd just get their fresh fruit and veg off him too.

He was a man who liked to dress well, and at this time he could afford to. He had a white Audi automatic with leather trim. We also had family membership of the Slieve Donard's new swimming pool, and I felt like something special, having this membership card to flourish. And it was because of the contacts he had at the Slieve Donard and elsewhere that, in 1970, Damian and I got to meet Celtic player David Hay and his friend Willie Carr. The two Scottish players had been staying at the Slieve in advance of an international match with Northern Ireland – the one in which George Best was sent off for throwing mud at the referee – and Dad had arranged for them to visit our house.

For a time Dad himself seemed cool in this new shop, because of a thing he used to do with the fella who delivered the chickens. I was there on occasion when the deliveries were made, and remember him saying, in his bravado, 'I'll toss you for them'. The way it worked was that Dad often asked for more than the telephone order, and he and the delivery man would gamble on the extra order – frequently dozens of chickens. If Dad won he got it for nothing; if the other man won, Dad paid him double – half to go back to the firm, and half for himself. I thought it was the coolest thing, seeing my father toss the coin in the air. One day, after Dad had won for a few weeks in a row, the van driver said that he'd like to toss the coin himself. Dad handed it to him, the coin was tossed, but Dad still won. I didn't realise at the time that he lost as much as he won; and I certainly didn't realise that gambling was a weakness in him and would be a source of conflict and misery.

When things were going well, Dad would invite some of his friends to the house on a Sunday evening. They would sit upstairs, in what we called the 'good room', and play cards. It was mainly poker, I think, and was definitely for money. Years later, Jimmy Murphy, who worked in Sawey's bookies at the time, told me about those days. It would start off fairly mild, apparently, but Dad and a few of the more serious gamblers would really push the pot. One time Dad threw the keys of the car in because he was short of cash. Someone in the company said, 'No, Pat, it's not worth that,' and returned the keys. But Dad put them back in, and played his hand, and he won. According to Jimmy, all the other men were relieved.

I often saw him sitting down the back of the shop with the racing pages when things were quiet, and he would ask certain men to put bets on for him when they were in town. I had no idea how much they were putting on for him but, when he had money, this gambling was a factor in all our lives.

He must have won some of the time, because one year, I think it was 1969, we had two holidays: Butlins, Mosney during the summer; and a Christmas holiday in the Ostan na Rosann hotel in County Donegal. That was unheard of for most of the ones I went to primary school with. Money didn't seem to be an object, and to the outside world Dad was a success – out at dinner dances regularly and involved with the Chamber of Commerce – but then we saw a different side to him than the world did.

In 1969, just as the Troubles were getting started, violence became a very regular occurrence in our own home. Mum would try to say her piece, often through tears. Then there would be fists and slaps. We would run to Mum to try to protect her, but be knocked out of the road, not even knowing what the argument was about. Then Dad would storm out and we'd be left trying to console Mum – the five of us, all under eleven. There was about a foot in height between our mum and our dad.

And, of course, in this time of hitting, I was hit myself. We all were – all the boys anyway. Sometimes if chores weren't done; or if I was at my homework when he came in from the shop and hadn't made the progress he'd expected. Instead of, 'Do you need a hand with that?', it would be a whack across the ear and the back of the head. But it's not just 'clips' I'm talking about. I can remember being hit on the side of the head so hard that it knocked me off my seat. My whole head was singing, my ear was sore, and there was blood on my lips. When this thing erupted in him, it was like a hurricane, and contrasted so sharply with the calm that descended when he'd gone. When he went out, you wouldn't have cared if he never came home.

And yet when he was high on the hog there could be good times – times when the storm was stilled so long that you forgot to be frightened. Ironically, one of those times was in the months before I was sent away to school – those summer months of 1970. Dad's moods were good, the weather was great and people were coming from all over the place for what we had in Newcastle – what was on our doorstep. The tills were ringing; Mum and Dad were in ceasefire mode; and football stars were making house calls on us.

Which only made being sent away from home even worse.

Chapter 3

ST COLMAN'S COLLEGE, VIOLET HILL, NEWRY

In those days in the north of Ireland, everyone did the 11-plus (the 'Qualifying'), a verbal reasoning test that determined whether you would go to the grammar school or a secondary. You could still go to a grammar if you failed it, but your parents had to pay.

I was promised a new bicycle if I passed it, but though I don't think I was that far off it, I didn't get the exam and I didn't get the bicycle. Then the conversations started, again above my head. Dad would say, 'He's going anyway. It'll be the making of him', which meant that I would be going to a Catholic boarding school – like other members of the town's Catholic quality and their children – whether I liked it or not. In Dad's eyes this was a matter of prestige. If it was good enough for our GP and his sons, it was going to be good enough for Patrick Gorman and his. And he put my name down for the nearest one – St Colman's College, Violet Hill, Newry.

Mum wasn't keen. She had no objection to the education end of it, but she didn't want me boarding. I was her first surviving child, and she'd always had her brood around her. Why could I not just come and go from school every day, like everyone else? Up to this point, apart from holidays and staying at my grandparents' or Auntie Betty's, I had never spent a single night away from home in my life. But Dad was adamant. There was no debate: 'This will make a man of him.'

I was really, constitutionally, unsuited to be a boarder. I know everyone starts at boarding school as an eleven-year-old, but I was a particularly *young* one, and particularly quiet. I didn't raise my small voice in opposition – not to Dad – but I did let Mum know exactly how I felt. She knew anyway, but she told me I wasn't to worry; everything was going to be all right. Very quickly after that I remember lists being made, and labels being ordered with my name on them, to be put on every item of clothing that I'd need. Mum went into that mode, but she reassured me constantly: 'Everything you need will be there for you and, no matter what, you'll be okay. It's a massive thing, I know, but don't be worrying.'

But I did worry, for I'd heard you didn't get home at weekends; it was only once a term.

A trunk arrived from Auntie Betty; a huge, big pirate-type thing, with dividers in it. And as that began to fill up, with clothes and sheets and blankets, the reality began to really hit home. I was not coming back any time soon, and that filled me with dread.

I visited the school once with Dad before I went there. My first impressions were of its massive size, and its gloom. Inside, the building was filled with sombre wood, and since

14

most of the staff were clergy, they were all in black. It seemed such a dark place, and everyone in it seemed dark.

On that day, we met the president of the school, Father Trainor. Once more the conversation was about me, above my head, and I wasn't part of it. This was adult stuff, and I was being 'sorted'. Fr Trainor seemed a nice enough man but he didn't ease my mind about any of the concerns consuming me. In the car on the way home with Dad there was no conversation, but a number of things were *relayed* to me: I was told how nice the president had been; how prestigious the school was; and how this had, clearly, been the right decision.

The clearest memory I have of my first day at school is of being in the dormitory: I was frightened (obviously) at the enormity of the move. I looked around, embarrassed, at the other boys as the place filled up. While some of them had big suitcases with them, nobody, but nobody, had a trunk. Mum hugged me before leaving and assured me I had everything I needed. There was a pat on the shoulder from Dad, and to be honest that's as much as I wanted. No one else was breaking down, so I didn't want to. I was trying, as everyone else was, to be a big boy.

My first contact, if you like, was with James, the boy in the next bed. He was from Leitrim, which wasn't that far away from us in Newcastle. But it might as well have been a hundred miles away, because I didn't know him. I knew no one.

After the families left, we were nearly all copying each other in our behaviour. Nobody broke down or screamed out the window. Jarlath Cushenan, the Dean, whose job was to look after us, came to show us the ropes. It was very practical. There was no, 'If you've ever any problems, boys, come to me.'

Whenever I think of the school, I go back to that dormitory. For this was one of the most alien things; this was the place that showed you how far you were from sleeping in your own bed. You were in a room with a couple of dozen other first years, strangers. Just beds and lockers; nothing curtained off; no privacy. Two senior boys slept at either end of our dormitory. They were there for lights out, to keep an eye on noise, that type of thing. Senior boys served us at mealtimes too, which was a strange thing. You wouldn't have dared say anything, but their slice of the cake – especially when actual cake was involved – was always bigger.

Everything was bigger. There were so many rooms in St Colman's College. So many corridors and stairways. The place was so *vast*. I had come from St Mary's Boys Primary School in Newcastle – at that time a tiny wee school with one corridor: classrooms to one side of it; toilets and cloakrooms to the other. You could open your classroom door and see everything in one go. But here there was so much to take in, you wondered if you ever would.

Then there was the regimentation, especially for boarders: 'You're going to the study hall now … You're going for your tea now … Going for prayers …' It felt a bit like being in prison: 'That's you. You get out when we say you get out.' In the early days, I felt completely on my own, and I was frightened. It was scary, enormously scary.

Yes, there were occasional Sunday visits from Mum, Dad or my brother Damian. Sometimes we'd go to Scappaticci's in Newry for fish and chips. But it wasn't every Sunday, and it was only for an hour or two. Mum would send me parcels of tuck, and letters – letters in which I could nearly hear her voice – and these things helped. I loved and hoarded those letters more than the tuck.

The biggest fella in our year was Seamus, and I made friends with him (as I was later to make friends with Eugene, the biggest boy in my year at St Louis). Seamus was big, but he was nice. Most of the staff were remote; they kept their distance. Francis Brooks – later Bishop Brooks – seemed very cross, and also scared me a bit because he had what we used to call a club foot. Most of the other teachers only seemed concerned with where you should be, and what you should be doing.

Very quickly the one who stood out as a friendly figure, who stood out above all the others, was the Religious Education teacher. All the teaching staff were men, and while some of them were okay, the one who would ask if *you* were okay – the only one, as far as I could see – was Fr Malachy Finegan.

Chapter 4

FINEGAN'S ROOM

I remember seeing Finegan first, before he spoke to me personally. He was in the distance with some boys and, whatever he was saying, the boys around him were laughing. He had stopped with them. He wasn't just giving commands and walking quickly away.

Finegan was a big man, physically a big man, and he was a big character. His exceptionally large ears had earned him the nickname 'Floppy'. He always smelled of cigarette smoke – off his clothes and off his breath. At times, too, you could smell drink off him.

As well as RE, he taught us Latin. The first time I remember him talking to me was outside of a classroom. There were two or three of us standing in a doorway, and he asked us how we were, how we were settling in – just talking, gentle talking. It wasn't like talking to Fr Trainor, the college president. Even if he had been saying the same things as Finegan, I wouldn't have known what to say to him. Finegan, at first, was like a friendly uncle. He used to come into our dormitory, the first-year dormitory, while we'd be getting undressed. At the time, I thought nothing of it; I had no fear in his company. I suppose I was comparing him to Dad, and I was comfortable, as a wee boy, when this charismatic big man stopped to talk to me. Maybe it even made me feel a bit special, I don't know.

While we'd had encounters in the corridors and around the grounds, the first time that I was invited to Finegan's room it was with another boy from my year. To this day I don't know if he was ever abused or has spoken about Finegan since, so I don't want his name coming from me. The boy had an older brother in second or third year, and he, along with a few others, were there the first time I went to the room.

I don't know of any other resident teachers who invited pupils to their rooms in this way. I never heard of it, and it certainly never happened to me with anyone else. But on that first occasion there was nothing untoward. It was just friendly, natural, 'how are you all getting on' type of chat. He might also have made a comment or two about what was on the TV (I remember watching *Magpie* there on subsequent days). It seemed nice. I felt welcomed. If anything, it was a wee taste of home.

Finegan's room was a sitting room (his other quarters, sleeping quarters, were somewhere else within the school). It was a couple of storeys up and had windows facing the playing fields and the long driveway. There was a sofa, a table, some comfortable chairs and a TV. There were a few books about it and some stuff on the walls, though to be honest I don't remember exactly what. When things changed, I spent an awful lot of time looking down.

But when things were innocent and nice – before he started doing things to me – I would look at the TV, or at the other boys when others were there. There'd always be an open bag of sweets, maybe Opal Fruits, on the table. I remember taking one the first time – being given permission, if you like, by one of the older boys doing so. I was still only eleven at the time.

The older boys seemed to know what to do and what to say; how to have general chit-chat in this room with this man. But I wasn't really nervous with him – as nervous as I would have been with Dad. And, in time, I began to contribute to the conversation myself. In fact it was more like a group of friends talking, with an adult chipping in. I did make a few friends at St Colman's, but I could also be on my own there quite a bit. Whether this made me susceptible to Finegan – or my particular size and look did – I neither know, nor really want to know. But I think there's a genius, an evil genius, in people like him that enables them to pick out and prey on the vulnerable. And I felt vulnerable at this time, and far away from home.

At no time did any kind of warning come to me from a bigger boy. Although I've heard since of brother-to-brother warnings concerning Finegan.

The first time he singled me out was at the start of November 1970. I was still eleven (I didn't turn twelve until 21 November). A group of us were leaving his room when he said to me, 'Come here till I see those eyes.' I didn't stay behind or anything that day, but he did put his arms around me and went on about how nice my eyes were, how blue. I haven't enjoyed a compliment about my eyes since. Some of the older boys who were there started calling me 'Little Owl' – I was small, and I did have big eyes – and that became my nickname at St Colman's.

That was the first time Finegan laid a hand on me, if you like. The first instance of abuse was also in his room. One day, I was running to the dormitory with other boys when he called me, just me, from his door. There was some of the usual chat at first, then he came over and sat beside me. I remember the big ears and head seemed to cut out the light as he came towards me. There was a kind of fumbling. Then he put his hand inside my shorts. I didn't understand what was happening. It was fumbling, like I say, and I just kind of froze. It was as if, big and all as he was, he had increased in size again. There was a lot of noise outside the room – a crowd of boys passing – and he stopped. I know he said something then, but I can't remember what. When I try to, I just hear something muffled. Then I was out. I went up to my friends, and it was weird. It was like a TV programme where you're suddenly zoomed out, then *whooshed* back to the place where you should be. When I met him next, which might have been the next day, he was no different than usual, not a bit. He was totally relaxed, totally confident. He always seemed to swan about in public.

The next time he had me in his room in private there was less chit-chat. He was over beside me right away. He got straight to it: started masturbating me and made me touch him. Again I didn't know what was happening; again I froze. He kissed me on the top of my head, on my hair – not my face.

Another time he seemed already excited and he pulled me towards his opened trousers. He put his hands around my head and pulled me to him. I remember scrunching my eyes and lips tight shut and feeling the front of him pushed towards my face.

As the abuse in his room went on, there were times when my own penis would be erect. But I had no idea what was happening to my body, or to me. He would talk to me sometimes – asking if I liked this or that – and I wouldn't know what to say or what to do. Occasionally he would give me money for the tuck shop. It annoys me now, more than I can really tell you, that I took it. But again, I didn't know what to do. I was so young.

I'm mad at myself about this now, too, but there remained some trace of the charismatic friendly uncle for me for some time; there were still occasional glimpses of 'kindness' in all the darkness – even though I understand now it was all for his own ends. For example, around my birthday, one of the prefects opened a special package from Mum to pick what he wanted from it first. I was being bullied by this bigger boy and was afraid of him. Just as he was opening my tuck parcel, Finegan walked in, in big-friendly-uncle mode, and gave off to him. The prefect gave back what he'd lifted, and Finegan said to me, 'If anything like that ever happens again, you come to me.' It was totally confusing, for I was frightened of the prefect and, even though what Finegan had begun to do to me was so much worse, I was glad of his intervention.

One day, Finegan saw me coming off the Gaelic football field and called me up to his room. This time he turned me round and pushed something into my bottom until it hurt. To this day, I couldn't tell you for certain if it was his fingers or his penis, but I cried out with the pain of it. I remember him pulling me towards him and hugging me then. The next day he gave me something, a present. It was a Dymo printer – a handheld device that allowed you to punch out words and short sentences. It was still in the box. I took it; for the want of knowing what else to do, I took it.

The Dymo, and the first rape, happened before Christmas 1970. I had just turned twelve.

I have two clear memories from my first trip home that Christmas after the abuse started. One was that the big surprise, the thing that I hadn't been told on the car journey back, was that we'd got our first ever colour television. I can remember distinctly that everyone was disappointed in my reaction, or lack of it. It was wonderful to see pictures in colour, but my excitement didn't manifest itself as they'd all have liked. Because of what else was in my head, I'm sure and certain: Finegan's TV, like everyone else's, was black and white.

The second memory is something from the journey back to school. There's a particular house between Hilltown and Mayobridge and, as I passed it that day, I thought, 'It won't be long now; I'm at the point of no return,' and I started counting. It took exactly eighteen minutes to get to the front of the school. Even to this day it registers with me that there's eighteen minutes from that house to the gates of St Colman's.

As he began to abuse me, I think some part of me shut it out, just to be able to function at the school, to survive. I was burying things as they were happening, just to get by. And I would bury them much more deeply as time went on.

Shortly after I returned from Christmas holidays, in the January of 1971, Finegan called me to his room. With little or no preamble, he started masturbating me. It was very fast and rough, as if he was in a hurry, as if he had to be somewhere else. At other times it was sort of slow and clumsy, but this time it was so fierce that it broke my foreskin, and it really, really hurt. I cried with the pain of it, and he gave me some money for the tuck shop, a heap of coins. I remember it was old money, and the new decimal money was just about to come in. I went up to the dorm feeling sore, worrying that people were looking at me.

The next time I saw Finegan, he just flowed down the corridor, untouchable. I never saw him going down the corridor any other way.

I desperately needed somewhere in the school where I could hide from him.

Chapter 5

A PLACE TO HIDE

Though it might not seem possible, after this the abuse got worse. All of it, *all of it*, stays with me, but one particularly unforgettable incidence occurred on a Saturday morning in the gym.

It was a sunny, dry morning and a group of us went down to play Gaelic on the pitch among ourselves. After a while, a crowd of the senior boys came down to train, and we moseyed off towards the front of the school, from where we could hear a lot of laughter. Some boys were watching friends of theirs playing in the handball alley and we went over too, but a persistent, drizzly rain started to fall, and everyone headed inside. Most of the boarders were there taking shelter from the rain, and we followed the main noise and ended up in the gym. There was a lot of messing going on, harmless fun, and there were balls, benches and ropes everywhere. We joined in – climbing ropes, jumping off benches, and kicking balls against the curtains on the stage.

I hadn't noticed that Finegan had come through the door until I heard him shouting at us. Most of the bigger boys had left by then, but me and my friends were having so much fun that we hadn't even heard him arrive. Finegan gave off about the mess and the fact that we shouldn't have been there and made us put everything back in its proper place – benches against the walls, ropes pushed back, and all the equipment returned in good order to the storeroom. When we were finished, Finegan told us that he didn't want to see us there again.

But when we were leaving, he asked me to stay and retrieve one ball that was still under a bench. I remember him saying something like I shouldn't be taking example from those other boys. I stumbled in the storeroom as I went to put the ball in its place and he said, 'Be careful.' He reached out to help me, and he hugged me. He told me he knew I was a good boy, and he kissed the top of my head. I remember the smell that was always about him, of cigarette smoke. I tried to pull away, but he squeezed me even tighter and pushed himself against me. I could feel his shirt sleeves, his bare arms, around my face, and I was frightened. He pulled my shorts and pants down and opened his own trousers. He started rubbing my penis and testicles and pressed himself against me harder. I could feel something pushing against my bottom. His arms were across my chest pulling me towards him, and I was crying because he was hurting me and he wasn't stopping. I felt this sharp pain, and his hands were still holding me tight. I couldn't move, but I could see his face beside mine. It was very red: the tops of his ears, his cheeks, the whole face crimson. I thought I was bleeding because I could feel that my bottom and my lower back was very wet.

He was mumbling something, I don't know what, and he was sweating. Then I remember him lifting the Irish tricolour from the storeroom, and wiping me and him down with it as if it were a towel. He told me not to cry; that I was okay; and that I was a good boy. He hugged me again and unlocked the gym door as we were leaving. I hadn't noticed him locking it in the first place. He told me to go out and enjoy that good day, something like that.

I remember walking up the corridor, hoping no one would notice that I'd been crying. Most people were outside, but I wouldn't go outside. I went up to the new secret hiding place I'd found and cried for my mum.

I'd known that I needed somewhere that he couldn't find me. I knew this when the sexual abuse started to physically hurt me. But even on the days when nothing happened, I'd started feeling abused. Looking back, I felt abused every day that I was under that roof. My radar was always active, watching out for him.

In the early days of being at the school, when we were running about investigating the place, I discovered that, in behind the blackboard of what I still think of as 'the big boys' study hall', there was a door. And through that door was a little space that was used as a store. There were boxes of books in it, bits and bobs, but that was all. It was above the chapel, open at one end, but it was safe.

In my mind, I was the only one who knew about this place. Which is crazy when you think about it – all the boys who used the study probably knew about it too. But what reinforced my trust in it as a place of sanctuary was that, in all the times I was in there, nobody ever opened the door – neither senior boy nor member of staff – so nobody asked what I was doing there, or told me to get out.

Finegan was a hard man to avoid, but I seemed able to do it in that space. And I started to go there on a Saturday if something had happened during the week. Even for a little while, to gather myself before joining my friends. And at times I would go to that wee place if I felt like talking to Mum, for I felt I could do it better there. I felt that she could 'hear' me better; that I was closer to her. And I suppose it was a kind of praying – in that something went out from me, and 'up'. What I told her was that bad things were happening, and I didn't want to be there. I wanted to be where she was, and my brothers and sister. But none of this ever leaked out into a letter. There was so much shame and distress, and I didn't have the language. Words failed me, if you like, but that place behind the blackboard never did. That half-forgotten storeroom defines the term *sanctuary* for me.

Chapter 6

NO PLACE TO HIDE

But I couldn't stay in my secret place forever. I had to move around the school, where Finegan was at large, walking around as if he were untouchable. As they'd say nowadays, he hid himself in plain sight.

He never once showed any contrition for what he'd done to me. Sometimes hours, even minutes, later he'd be out and about again, chatting. That was confusing to me. How could he do that? But what was worse was that I could respond to the avuncular character whenever he reappeared. I hated myself for it, but he could draw me into that other version of himself. He deployed that skill as a tool of his abuse.

But over time, Finegan became less careful, even reckless. Maybe he thought that he'd never be caught, or that it wouldn't matter if he was. He would call me off the Gaelic pitch when he felt like it. It was becoming routine, casual, entitled. Like this one incident that happened outside – not in a corner, not in his room. It was the weekend, and there wasn't a wealth of things for boarders to do at the weekends. We used to congregate round the handball alley and watch other boys playing, if we weren't playing ourselves. I was in the alley and saw something that I'd never seen before, nor since: two boys standing very close to each other, spitting. They were having a duel; loading whatever phlegm they could from the back of their throats and hurling it at each other. The winner was going to be whichever one could stand there longest.

We weren't there very long before Finegan came out. He stopped it immediately and the two boys involved were sent in to be dealt with. In the open, as everyone was dispersing, he told me not to be associating with boys like that (as was his wont) and he touched my privates with his hand, over my clothes. It was no accident for, as I flinched and turned away, he patted my bottom. My main concern was that I hoped no one had seen *me* – as if *I* had done something wrong.

No one said anything that day, but I can't swear that no one saw anything. The dean, Jarlath Cushenan, for example, who was here, there and everywhere all the time. We used to joke that there were two of him.

In February 1971, I was supposed to go to see Manchester United playing Spurs. George Best was playing; and Pat Jennings on the other side. I had been looking forward to it with all my heart, but in the week running up to the match I caught a bug and was taken out of daily routine at the school. I was brought over to the infirmary and put in isolation under the care of Sister Mel and Sister Euphrasia. I was there no time before Finegan came in. He was sitting on my bed, asking how I was, when – hot on his heels – the dean appeared. Now was that deliberate? Was it coincidence?

Had Cushenan told himself that Finegan needed watching? Either way, the 'jolly uncle' persona disappeared very quickly and Finegan didn't sit on. The two men left together.

I saw Cushenan again on the last day that I was abused. And he saw me.

Again it was a weekend, and people were milling about outside. A car pulled up at the far end of the drive and the driver and passenger, one of the senior boys, swapped places. The car then sped up the drive in a show of bravado. It skidded and hit the wall at the front of the school.

My first reaction was fear – I didn't want to be questioned as a witness to what had happened and who was involved. So I scarpered; I went into the school and up to the dormitory. There was nobody else there, but Finegan soon appeared. Without saying anything at all, he started to abuse me. His hands went into my pants, and he pulled them down. He started to masturbate me as he undid his own trousers.

At that point, Cushenan came in, and again I have to wonder why. But there is absolutely no doubt at all about what he would have seen. He would have clearly seen his colleague and fellow priest masturbating me. My clothes were pulled down; my genitals and everything were exposed. Cushenan said something like, 'What's going on here?', and there was a heated conversation – another conversation that was above my head. At first, I just stood there, and then I pulled my clothes back up. I can't remember what exactly passed between them, but the two men left the dormitory together, and neither man ever made any reference about it to me.

That incident, which was just after Easter 1971, was the

last time I was abused by Fr Malachy Finegan. He left the school at the end of that term, which was the end of the school year.

He served for two years in Newry parish, before returning to the staff of St Colman's in the autumn of 1973. He went on to serve as president of the college from 1976 until 1987.

Chapter 7

BACK HOME

I was so relieved to be back home for the summer, and I was determined that I would be home for good.

As well as reconnecting with my family, I reconnected with my friends. Some of us – me, Micky, Dicker and Seamy Mental – tried to get a band together. There was a lot of entertainment on in St Mary's, our parish hall – things like pantomimes, 'nights at the races' and the annual ballad festival. I used to take part in the pantomimes, in the chorus, but the ballad festival seemed to be at another level – with individuals and small groups performing like on *Top of the Pops*. Me and Micky first had the notion to enter, thinking that it could be a stepping-stone to bigger things. But to hell with just taking part, we thought, let's win the thing! Dicker and Seamy could accompany us on keyboards and drums (maybe), while me and Micky, who were the driving forces behind the band, would be the Lennon-and-McCartney. We'd organise the rehearsals, and we would source the songs.

A lot of LPs in the radiogram in the good room upstairs were by Jim Reeves, José Feliciano and Count John

McCormack. There was the odd James Young album, but none of those served our purposes. We tried writing down the lyrics from songs we heard on the radio, but that was too stressful. The song would be over before you'd caught enough of the words, and it could be the next day before it came round again. But then one of us got hold of BJ Thomas's 'Hooked on a Feeling', and we were away. It took a lot of lifting and laying of the stylus to get the whole thing transcribed – especially the 'Ooga-Chaka, Ooga-Chaka' of the intro – and a steady hand not to damage the record with the needle, but we hadn't one between us.

Now that we had our material, all we needed was a name. We knew it had to be something catchy to launch our career. And one day Micky arrived at our house drinking a bottle of Fanta. If I'm not mistaken it was lemon rather than orange, which was even more exotic. It was a lightbulb moment and 'Micky and the Fanta' was born. We were ready to enter the competition, except … we didn't. As it got nearer the time, we just kind of chickened out.

But the sun was shining outside, it was summer, and I was home. I had this dark thing on the inside, but along with it, my determination – or fierce hope – that I was done with St Colman's. The problem, of course, was Dad. He was a religious man, a daily communicant, and had a great respect for the priests and institution of the Catholic Church. Not only was he set on me being a pupil at a prestigious Catholic school, but had I the words to even begin telling him the sort of things that had happened, I was sure I would be punished for telling 'lies' about one of God's anointed.

I didn't have the words. Not even to tell Mum, although I did tell her that I was being bullied – bullied to the extent that I simply could not go back. Anytime I'd talk to her about it, I'd be in tears. I think that if it had just been me and her dealing with this, the truth might have come out, but it was a struggle, always a struggle, talking to Dad.

Thankfully, at the time St Louis, a local convent school, had just started to take boys. Since it was run by nuns, Mum and I both thought that there was at least a chance that Dad would go along with it. He wasn't a bit happy, but he didn't say an outright no and the involvement of nuns gave us something to chip away with. It was a real fight though, and the brunt of the battle was borne by Mum.

However over the summer the decision was made that I could go to St Louis. I was absolutely over the moon, and so relieved. My attitude was, *I know that they're nuns, but they're also women. And women won't hurt me – Mum's a woman.*

Over that summer of '71, things between Mum and Dad really deteriorated. It had obviously been happening when I wasn't there too, and I think I missed it, initially, in the excitement of being back home, but it became apparent, very quickly, that there were massive cracks between them. The rows were constant, and the violence more frequent and intense until one day, just before the schools went back from the summer break, Mum packed a suitcase and went to her sister, Auntie Betty, in Dromore. From the elation of not having to go back to St Colman's, I found myself down again – right down at the bottom of the hill. Not knowing anything about gambling – and clearly not knowing anything about adult relationships – I thought Mum and Dad had broken up entirely because of me. All I knew was that before I went away things were reasonably calm, and there was turmoil when I came back.

I was kept home with Dad because I was enrolled now at St Louis; Damian was kept at home too, to do the 11-Plus; but the younger three ended up in Auntie Betty's small house, with her and Mum. At first, all of us kids were at home with Dad, and he used to leave the younger ones at Auntie Betty's for occasional visits. But soon there was so much tension between Mum and Dad that there was room for nothing else, and Dad used to just leave them at the top of the street, and later, when it was time to collect them, gun the car away when Mum was waving them off. One time after a visit, at a signal from Brendan (the oldest of the young ones), all three bailed out as the car was moving off. Brendan cut his knees, calling to mind Mum's cut knees in Tullybrannigan. She ran out and gathered the three of them in. They stayed with her from that point and went to school in Dromore.

Damian would visit some weekends and was put up by a neighbour of Auntie Betty's. I visited less frequently because there wasn't room in the neighbour's house for both of us. But Mum sometimes came to visit me. It was a few weeks after she'd left, and I hadn't seen her since, when I was in one of the prefabs at the front of my new school and I saw a car coming up the drive. One of the boys said, 'I think that's your mother,' and I was embarrassed, because none of the other boys' mothers were coming to see them in school. I was called out of class, and Mum took me for lunch in a cafe in Kilkeel owned by the father of a friend of mine. Mum's brother, my uncle Eugene, was with us too. This happened a few times – obviously the nuns knew the story – and I was told, each time, that I wasn't to tell my Dad.

I told none of my friends that my parents, and family, were separated. The boy who'd said 'I think that's your mother' said it another time and I told him that it was an aunt of mine who was emigrating – a woman who looked like my mother, but wasn't her. I didn't know anyone else whose parents were split up, and I didn't want the stigma. But while Newcastle was a small town, it's not a thing I was ever teased about.

I'd started St Louis in second year – which was also the second year they'd ever taken boys. And literally overnight I kicked off. The quiet, shy boy who didn't want to be noticed (but had been, by Malachy Finegan), changed completely. I think at that time the nuns were a bit unsure how to deal with boys. They called assemblies where there would be uniform inspections for the boys – to check, like in an army, that we were wearing our gear correctly. (The girls told us that this never used to happen to them.) It wasn't big stuff, but I embraced any chance at all for rebellion. They told us to wear dark socks, so I made sure mine were multicoloured – the sort that Slade were wearing. I wore platformed soles and painted each shoe a different colour, hoping, willing, to be called for inspection that day.

I grew my hair longer than allowed, and got my ear pierced. Rebelling all the time – and leading from the front in any rebellion. If they said go left, I'd go right; if they said black, white. What's the worst thing that could happen? The staff were mostly women and if you were sent to Sister Dorothy, the principal ... well, okay. I'd felt so damaged and oppressed in the other school, and here was a chance to fight back. Nuns were in the same gang, if you like, as priests, but were women, and they wouldn't hurt me.

I got a name, fairly quickly, among the staff and my fellow pupils. If anyone noticed a change in me at home, and I don't think they did, there was nothing said.

There was only me, Dad and Damian at home now in any case. But in the final months of 1971 and into '72, other people appeared on the scene – Mrs McCrum and her children. I was old enough to know to some extent what this meant, and I hated it. Mrs McCrum (not her real name) was a widow, and her two children, a boy and a girl, were a bit younger than us. She was from Lisburn, the same town as Dad, and I think he'd known her husband. He was obviously fond of her, but I was devastated, and it made me miss Mum more. I was frightened; too frightened of Dad to say anything about it, but I asked myself, *Does this mean that's it? Half of us here, and half of us somewhere else? Is that the way it's always going to be?*

One thing I was absolutely sure about – Mrs McCrum would never be our mum. As things progressed between her and Dad, they took Damian and me and her two kids on a short break to Bray. It must have been around Halloween 1971. The idea was that we were to be, or act like, a family. I remember Dad saying to me and Damian, 'There's something I want you to do. While we're staying here, call Mrs McCrum "Mum".' I said I wouldn't. I just said it, straight out, by instinct, without counting the cost. Dad drew the back of his hand across my face. Mrs McCrum told him to leave it: 'It's all right, Pat.'

That Christmas there was another attempt to bring the two families together when Dad and Mrs McCrum took us to the Ostan na Rosann in Donegal ... the same place we'd been with Mum and the younger children in the Christmas of 1969. And maybe it was because we'd been here before with our own family that it wasn't a success. It was just so poignant and sad for Damian and me. Dad would say things like, 'You're going to enjoy this – whether you like it or not!' and he was being serious. Mrs McCrum tried – I think she tried hard – to be nice to us, but we really didn't want to be there at all, and there was no remedy for that.

After that Christmas, the Troubles visited us in our quiet corner of the North. On 23 January 1972, one week before Bloody Sunday, there was a march from Castlewellan to Newcastle. The march had been banned, but the organisers decided that it would go ahead anyway, as would the rally in Donard Park where Bernadette Devlin and others were to speak. I hadn't a great awareness of the Troubles yet, but the show was coming to our town that day, and Micky, myself and a few friends from St Louis arranged to meet up. Dad was away somewhere, so I didn't have to answer to him. There was a strong police and army presence, and a lot of movement from them, but events really exploded when, coming back from Donard Park, the people were stopped at the bridge. The authorities had obviously decided that this march back from the rally was going no further.

When the army blocked the road, people went down to the beach and gathered rocks and stones. The next thing, there were tear gas canisters flying through the air. We did what everyone else was doing … or maybe the half of it, because although we lifted stones and lumps of rock, we didn't throw them. At least, *I* didn't anyway. I was frightened by the people running towards us, clearly affected by the CS gas. It was getting hard to breathe, even for us. Soon we were fighting for breath and could hardly see, so I said we should try to get into our house, by the back way.

We ran then, and one of us fell. He was picked up and put on his feet by two adults who didn't seem to break stride. We fell into the safety of the back yard, coughing and spluttering. When we got into the house and threw water round our faces, it seemed, initially, to make things worse. But to us, who were just into our teens, we knew that something big had happened and we hadn't just watched it on the TV – we had been there. We may not have been at the forefront of anything that day, but we had sampled something. And the taste of it was strong.

Chapter 8
ON THE MOVE

'So, you're moving to Australia,' I was informed one day in school. The girl who said this was from Newcastle too and must have heard something in her house before I had in mine, as she was right: it was early 1972, and Dad had plans to move us all – me and Damian, along with Mrs McCrum and her two – halfway round the world. A banner appeared in the shop window: 'Owner Emigrating – Everything Must Go'.

It was a shock, the sort of shock that's hard to absorb. Our home and shop were going to be sold. But this wasn't a calm ordering of affairs before the start of a new life. The bank had ordered the sale, and it wasn't a good time to sell (the house and shop eventually went for just £9,000, or so I was told; and the auction for fixtures and fittings in the shop was a disaster). We didn't understand what was going on. How could we? Damian and I had been drilled to tell certain callers that Dad wasn't in; but as children, you do what's asked of you; you do what you're told. At our age, we knew nothing about banks or crippling debt.

Everything was starting to crumble for Dad and it was happening very quickly – he'd lost his marriage, his business and his home (though the new owners allowed us to stay on for a while after the sale). The dream of Australia (a nightmare for us) also disappeared, as did Mrs McCrum.

It was at this stage, around Easter, that Mum and the wee ones came back. They arrived one Sunday afternoon, and me and Damian were excited. But we weren't sure if this was a visit, or something more. Mum and Dad went up to the good room, by themselves, to talk. The five of us were gleeful, and a wee bit over-exuberant. It's funny what stays with you, but I remember that *Mr Piper* was on the TV in the background and its theme tune was 'Come with me and you'll see/All the wonders there will be …'

After what seemed like an age, Mum and Dad came back down the stairs, and Dad said, 'We're going to give it another go.' Mum was standing behind him, smiling at us as he spoke. I remember the joy breaking out of us; the leaping around. We were all back together in our big house and shop now. Though the fact was we owned neither any more, and were literally on borrowed time there.

Then, just a few short weeks after the homecoming, Dad had a breakdown.

It's hard to pinpoint when exactly this happened, but it was as if, with Mum back, he *could* break down. He seemed to start to unravel – to lose his 'tightness' and control – and, having started, he didn't stop. His behaviour became even more unsettling. He seemed ill-at-ease and lost all the time – it's hard to explain.

He went into the Downshire mental hospital at the start of the summer. Mum, Damian and I would go and visit, and he'd be very argumentative. For all his aggression, Dad wasn't someone who cursed, but now he would turn the air blue, f-ing and blinding in his dressing gown. Each visit ended up in the Sugar Bowl, the patients' cafe where my mind would work overtime, trying to think of something to say.

I seemed to be encountering a lot of things that carried stigma: the secret I was holding inside me; the splitting-up of my parents; and the fact that my Dad was in what everyone called 'The Mental'.

As soon as he got out, another thing came along: we moved out of our big house on Main Street and went to live in a caravan. And although there was a bus stop outside Sunnyholme (the caravan park), when school started again, I would walk back up the Castlewellan Road to get the bus at the station. I didn't want anyone to know I didn't live in a house, so I used to get dropped off at the station in the afternoon too.

When we first went to the caravan park there were other people there, it was still summer. But quickly we became the only residents, and that was strange. As autumn arrived, we shared the site with only one other, occasional, occupant. Who apparently – though I never saw him myself – was Ian Paisley.

We had gas mantle light, no TV, and the place was hard to heat. As winter crept in, it was a pain to have to walk to the toilet block to wash in the morning. I can remember my own foot- or slipper-prints in the frost. And at night we slept in the same place that we ate and did everything else in the day. It was tough.

Dad would just sit there for long periods being very, very quiet. But Mum wasn't hiding away. She'd be up the town, doing the messages, with her head held high, and talking to everyone. Without her I don't know what we would have done. She took a job doing the dishes in the back of the Savoy cafe, and she cleaned for a couple of better-off people in the town. If she had anything to swallow to do that, she swallowed it whole.

People gave us a hand at this time when we were so far down, especially family. Just before we'd left Main Street, a deposit had been paid for me to go on a school trip to Paris. I was sure that, when we moved to Sunnyholme, I wouldn't be able to go, but Auntie Betty stepped in and said, 'You absolutely will be going!' Whatever was left to be paid, she paid, and I set off for the City of Lights from a caravan site. There were also regular letters from Auntie Anna, another sister of Mum's, each containing folding money, and even then I knew how vital these were to us.

I had no regrets at all when we were able to leave the caravan. I longed to get back into a homeplace that wasn't on wheels. It wasn't the novelty for me that it maybe was for the younger ones, and I was delighted to hear we'd got a bricks-and-mortar house near the Donard Park. Oliver King (our milkman, and a friend of Dad's) moved us, our possessions and our dog in his flat-back lorry. And Sister Gonzaga, a local nun, helped us unload and settle in. The place was simply furnished – but nothing to be ashamed of

– and I was relieved I could now say to my friends, 'Sure call at the house.'

We were only there one night.

As we were upstairs excitedly arguing about rooms, the owner arrived. His visit started off okay, but when he saw there was a nun there – two nuns by this stage – something must have gone off in his head. We very quickly got the sense that he wasn't happy with a Catholic family moving in. He said something about not realising there were children, never mind a dog – but I remember my parents dismissing that out of hand. No children allowed? Wasn't one of the bedrooms a wee girl's room? And hadn't another got bunk beds in it for little ones?

Whatever about that, he gave us one night – not two, or to the end of the week, but one night to find somewhere else.

The disappointment in me was every bit as strong as the excitement about moving home had been – it was probably stronger. And witnessing my parents' handlessness before what they'd experienced as blatant sectarianism left its mark. Years later my best friend, Micky, had to talk me out of setting fire to a climbing plant at the back of that house.

We needed a roof over our heads, and there was a scramble about where we would go. The feelers went out – through the nuns, through the contacts my parents had – and we got one: a house called, of all things, 'Walton', on the Shimna Road. It was a refuge, and we were like refugees – refugees who had a place now: 'Yes, you can stay here.' Once again, Oliver moved us. And once again I looked forward to settling in.

So much had happened to me in the past year or so that

if I ever stopped to think about it, my head spun until I felt sick. So I tried not to think about it – what had happened to the family; what had happened to me – and to just keep moving. I was always at or up to something.

Unlike the Waltons, we only stayed in our new place for a few months.

Chapter 9

RAILWAY STREET

It is maybe ironic that the next place we moved to was above a bookies. The accommodation in Railway Street had fallen vacant, and Dad was friendly with the owner, the bookie. Compared to Walton, which was very small, it was a rung back up the ladder towards the kind of place we'd had to leave in Main Street. (Which, in a further irony, now houses a bookies.)

I liked the house; I think we all did. It too was only a short-term let, but it was the first place in which I saw a bit of Dad's morale coming back. It wasn't a miraculous transformation or anything, but he did start to go out and up the street again. And Oliver King paid his dues so he could go to the Mourne Golf Club. Dad also started to take more care of his appearance again – a thing he'd always been noted for.

And in the middle of 1973, at fourteen and a half, I was taking care of mine. Parallel trousers and Crombie coats were the height of fashion, and there was a market beside us in Railway Street where Mum could source the affordable versions. I wore my 'Crombie' with pride, pulling the red lining out of the top pocket for a touch of class. Flapping up the street in my parallels and coat, there was no one like me. For the first time in a long time I'd say that life felt good. I'd started to hang out in the Broadway Cafe with my friends, and I had a part-time job in another cafe – the Imperial – beside our old house and shop.

I was working there the night that the Railway Street bomb went off.

Next door to the bookies and our house was Sydney Jay's shop. It sold a bit of everything, and he and his family lived above it. He had formerly been a member of the B-Specials, an auxiliary police force, and on the evening of Saturday, 21 July 1973, a bomb was left in the doorway of his shop and a warning shouted.

Our Mum received a warning too, directly from the bombers. They had driven away at speed from the shop but pulled up beside her as she was talking to Auntie Betty from a phone box at the corner (we didn't have our own phone then). One of the occupants shouted, 'Mrs Gorman, is there anyone in the house?' When she said yes, she was told to get everyone out – the back way. I don't think he gave any more details, and the car sped off. Everyone – the Jays and all the Gormans bar me – were safely out the back before the bomb exploded.

The ones who had planted it had another bomb in their car but it exploded prematurely as they drove to another place in the town – a place that was used socially by off-duty soldiers. Two of the people in the car were killed – one of them the man who had warned our Mum, and his fiancée. That explosion happened outside the Broadway Cafe, which I'd just started to frequent.

No one could get a hold of me, and Mum was sick with worry. The whole family was. Mum was convinced that I'd come home from the Imperial and gone in the back entry, not realising the danger. It was only when my shift was over and I appeared at the security force cordon that everyone knew I was safe.

Of course there was an element of fear when we went inside the house later that night: the Jays' house had been wrecked by the bomb. But, oddly, very little damage was done to ours. We didn't need builders to come and repair anything, and in very little time we were able to move in again. As someone not fifteen years of age, I was impressed. Such a degree of thought had gone into the operation, I believed, that they'd worked out how to destroy next door but leave our windows intact. I do remember one man looking round the relative lack of damage upstairs in our house, and saying to my Dad, 'The boys knew what they were doing, Pat …'

For many days afterwards the town was in a state. There were police and army and forensics people all over the place. Many shops didn't open again until the following week, and the awful death that the two young people had had hung over everything. It was a shock – there's no doubt about that – to our quiet town. And there was a sense of disarray that lasted for some time.

As did the thought – the romantic thought in me – that one of those who'd lost their lives had warned us personally.

Chapter 10

MOURNE RISE

There were houses under construction out the Castlewellan Road – out towards the caravan park – and we wanted one very badly. We needed a decent base, a proper home. We'd been bouncing around short-term lodgings for too long. When the new houses were nearing completion, Dad walked across a plank over a trench on the site and pushed a Miraculous Medal through one of the doors. The prayer, of course, was that we'd be given one of the houses, but in the first allocation we weren't – to our great disappointment. Then one of the families that had received a house moved on very quickly, and we were allocated 5 Mourne Rise, the house on the corner ... the very one that Dad had posted the Miraculous Medal into.

Once again, we arrived on the milk lorry, only this time with some of the things that we hadn't seen since Main Street. It was a Housing Executive house, a rented house, but it was ours. No one was going to come by in two weeks or two months and say that we had to move again. It was ours. It was *ours*, and we could not be moved.

This is where we all spent most of our teenage years.

As a teenager, there is no doubt that I was reckless – two kinds of reckless: what you might call 'ordinary reckless' and 'Northern Irish reckless'. Under 'ordinary' you could put something like playing truant; under 'Northern Irish', the Troubles kind of trouble I got into later.

The father of one of our gang, Seamy, had a caravan that he only rented out in the summer months. All the rest of the year it lay vacant outside the house, which suited us nicely. Seamy's father went round the country selling clothes and boots to farmers with limited access to shops. He'd be up early to load his big estate car, and we would lie under the caravan in our uniforms until he was away. We would then use the spare key that was hidden under a slab that one of the wheels sat on, and spend the day at our leisure. Eventually we were caught and had to do every repair under the sun for him not to tell our parents.

Then, when I was about fifteen or sixteen, I used to take Dad's car – talk about baiting the bear! When he'd go for a walk or up to the club, I, without having had a driving lesson in my life, would take the motor jumping, stalling and bouncing around the estate. At first, I would just take the keys to turn the car on, then put them back; as I grew cockier, I would reverse up and down the drive to the car port; but, when I was sixteen, I thought I'd take it a bit further. I had a girlfriend now – Deirdre Doran from the nearby village of Dundrum – and I decided I would surprise her with a visit. The car humped, bumped and jumped the whole way along the road. I thought, 'This is great. I can drive now.'

When I pulled up outside Deirdre's, her mother nearly had a heart attack, and told me to, 'turn round and take that car home straight away!' Inevitably when I got home, Dad was standing in the drive with Mum explaining frantically that I was just around the corner ... He took the keys with him every single time after that.

In the summer of '75, when I was sixteen, I got a job in the Arcadia amusements. Micky and I were bingo callers there – Pongo callers actually. For Pongo, you'd put a 5p piece into a machine, the screen would light up and you would flick doors closed over the numbers that had been called. Micky and I would take turns between working on the rostrum and walking among the punters. 'Take a seat and rest your feet and have a game of Pongo!' was our cry. And it could be heard up and down Main Street via speakers on the outside of the building, drawing in the customers. One of the people who used to come in was Deirdre. This was how we met – we had clicked. Very soon we were an item, and I used to 'help' her babysit at her sister Mairead's house, just round the corner from our own.

Having the job also meant I had a reason to stay home, alone, when the rest of the family went on a short holiday late in the summer.

I was old enough to be trusted now, apparently.

As sure as night follows day, this led to a house party. The lads were there – I'm not sure if Deirdre was – and so were some of their brothers and their friends. We had the stereo speakers out in the front garden blasting away. We fired the barbecue inside the house and passed the food out. Dad was selling fish again from a custom-made trailer, and there were freezers in the garage full of scampi and fish and all sorts. At least, they *were* full before the house party started. Salmon steaks, baskets of chips and meatballs all made their way from the kitchen. And some of the older ones were able to organise a carry-out.

Everyone was sitting in the garden, as large as life, in front of the neighbours, when Dad, being Dad, came back a day early to try to catch me out. I was rustling up another feed in the kitchen when someone said, 'That's your da pulling up.'

'Ha, ha,' said I, 'He's not back until tomorrow.'

But it was him, and all the fellas in the garden fled like snow off a ditch. There was only one door in that house – at the front – and other fellas flew out the back windows. Micky was the only one to stay, but then he had to go too.

I got everything. And I was banned from everything … *for life!*

Although there was maybe some change since his time in the hospital, things could still be very dark with Dad. Because of what had happened to me, I wasn't keen on the Church, but I lived in a house where you didn't only have to go to Mass, you had to go to everything: Benediction, Stations of the Cross … whatever you're having yourself. It wasn't like that for any of my friends, and it could lead to embarrassment. And, occasionally, something that went far beyond embarrassment.

One weekend, James, a friend of mine from school, was

staying over in Mourne Rise. We went to Mass on the Sunday morning, but that wasn't enough for Dad. He said that there was Benediction on in the afternoon.

I said we had plans.

'Plans? What plans?'

'Just heading up the town.'

Mum said that was all right, but Dad said it wasn't a bit all right.

'You and your friend, as long as you're under my roof, are going to Benediction if I say you're going to Benediction.'

In fairness to him, he had no idea that the pomp and ceremony of the like of Benediction made me think of Finegan.

I held my ground and refused to go. 'No we're not, Da.'

And, in front of James, he hit me.

Contrast that with a visit I made to my friend Eugene's home. We did go to Mass on the Sunday (though we didn't have to go to anything else), but the night before, while we were watching TV, Eugene's father asked him and his brother and me for our shoes. And he sat at the fireside and polished them.

What James had witnessed in our house was, there was Benediction on, and we were going. I refused and *Bang*. What I witnessed in Eugene's house was laughter, fun: 'Do you want another slice of cake?' and, 'Gimme, I'll polish your shoes.'

I thought it was a lovely thing, a beautiful thing to do.

Chapter 11
REBEL, REBEL

Looking back now, I'd connect my newfound teenage recklessness with Finegan. Recklessness itself became a kind of sanctuary for me. It was a place for me to go. It was 'who I was' to my mates, for I was rasher than them; rasher than a 'normal' teenager. It was like, if I did x or y to the absolute limit, I could build the wall high enough for what had happened to me not to get through. I was doing these other things to try to wipe it out. But it was a shell, a hard shell to protect what was inside. I was going round with my mates – my gang now – and there was safety in that. And one sure thing about St Colman's was I hadn't been safe there.

As a teenager out looking for a spot of bother and a sense of belonging, there was no better place to be than in 1970s Northern Ireland, with its Troubles. I couldn't help becoming more conscious of them at that time. The Loyalist Workers' Strike of 1974 meant that sometimes we couldn't get to school; and at other times the army and police would come on to the bus. It was nothing like Derry or Belfast, but

I was aware that things were happening, and I wanted to be part of them.

Some of the older ones – teenagers and young adults – set up Newcastle Anti-British (NAB) and I gravitated towards and grasped at the sense of fellowship it offered. We started with small stuff – breaking windows and spraying graffiti in the name of NAB – but I thought, *This is what you do; this is how you fight back.*

I began to sneak out of the house at night to paint graffiti, then I'd volunteer to phone in bomb-scares, in order to create trouble at which we could pelt the army. Even in the company of the older ones I'd put myself forward. There wasn't an oath, as such, but you were told in no uncertain terms not to be saying anything, except what you were told to say, if you were caught. If I knew something was going to happen, I'd be there – even ahead of the rest of my friends. I didn't have the same fear or worry of getting caught by the police. Maybe because of this real hurt I'd had; this really bad and personal thing that had happened to me, I'd think, *Fuck it, like. What's the worst thing that could happen now?*

Some of NAB's operations were serious, and some were less so. Like the time we attacked the bowling green, for Ireland. The bowling green was managed by the council, so was a symbol of the establishment and a 'legitimate target'. The council took great pride in the green's appearance, and always cut the grass to within an inch of its life. We thought about going in the dead of night to cut the letters NAB into it, but that was rejected as too lengthy and vulnerable a procedure. Then someone suggested we could burn the

57

letters into the surface with bleach. So that's what we did.

The damage was not immediately clear and distinct, so we went back for days afterwards, looking for the effects to appear, thinking, *This'll stop the bowling; this'll give them pause for thought.* But the results were disappointing, barely visible at all. We must have used one of the lesser, 'own brand' bleaches.

When I was fifteen or sixteen, a friend of mine liberated a starting pistol from his school. We were wondering how best to use it, when an opportunity presented itself. The scouts were organising a gathering in Tipperary Wood outside the town, and we saw them – the Baden-Powell Scouts – as a symbol of the invader. So we thought we'd use the starting pistol to 'drive them off the land'. There were three of us, and we went along the river's edge until we found ourselves opposite their campsite. They were gathered around a campfire, singing their 'Ging-Gang-Goolie' and roasting a pile of sausages. I said, 'Give the pistol to me,' and I went down to the river to scare the scouts off in the name of the Republic.

I stepped into a clearing and waved the pistol at them to attract their attention. But all they saw was the waving, and they waved back at me. This went on for some time, back and forth: me trying to express that, no, I wasn't trying to greet them but to drive them from the land, but to no avail. There was no persuading them that they were being expelled. And there are times when you just have to fold your tent and leave the field.

I was brought up to the police station a few times for

breaking windows and firing catapults, that type of thing. Each time, they happened to call at the house when Dad wasn't there, so Mum was able to come with me and keep it from him. She just seemed able to mop up trouble. She was always doing it. I can't honestly say how that affected her, but I know that I didn't want to add too much to her burdens (even though I did add to them). Which is probably one reason I didn't tell her what had happened at St Colman's.

It was a bit frightening, as you can imagine, to be in a police station, but I wasn't frightened of them, I was frightened of what Dad would do if he heard about it. I was more afraid of him than of any particular situation I was in. And I did get into situations that could have had grave, even fatal, consequences.

Even in a town like Newcastle, the police and army patrolled regularly, and we used to fire stones at them but, when we got the starting pistol, I took that to another level. One night, in 1974 I think, we were in a lane beside the hardware shop in the town – ironically the lane my family had used in July the previous year, on the night of the bomb. It afforded access to Main Street at one end and various routes of escape at the other. We thought that, if we pulled out the starting pistol, we could give a police or army patrol some fuckin' fright. Now it was just that, a starting pistol: no one was going to get shot.

I volunteered to fire the pistol and went to the top of the lane where it meets Main Street. This is near a corner, where any oncoming vehicle would have to slow down to turn. The first few nights that I waited there, nothing came.

But not too many evenings went by before the shout went up that there was a police Landrover coming. As it came round the corner, I stepped out of the dark alleyway and fired the starting pistol at it. The Landrover swerved and we ran along the route we had planned. It wasn't until afterwards, years afterwards, that I thought very hard about what could have happened that night – to whoever was in that vehicle, and to me. The Landrover could easily have crashed, injuring its occupants and other people, and I – as a dark figure stepping out with a 'gun' – could have been shot dead.

Chapter 12
SMARTS' FRONT ROOM

The path that I was on with NAB could have led to a darker place. There was a progression, if that's the right word, for young people on both sides during the Troubles – from footering around in youth and other organisations, to the serious stuff. What definitely saved me from that was the time I spent in the front room of Susan Smart's house.

For about three years in the mid-70s – from I was fifteen to nearly eighteen – this was the most important place in the world to me. It came about because, at that time, prior to the years when we'd be going to pubs, I used to hang out in the Broadway Cafe with Micky, Dicker and Seamy. The Broadway was one of the two cafes in the town owned by the Paolinelli family and winter or summer, you'd find us moored around a table for as long as we possibly could, and for the smallest possible outlay. Arthur and Lido Paolinelli were fairly tolerant, but if one of them saw us sitting with nothing in front of us for just too long, we'd be asked to leave.

After eking out the one portion of chips or single Coke for as long as humanly possible, I used to unscrew the vinegar bottle and sup at it for something to do. That's how I got the nickname 'Vinners', which many people still use for me.

The Broadway held many attractions for fellas our age – the jukebox, the craic and the girls who worked there. There was also a small group of girls around our own age, Susan Smart, Beverly and Monica, who seemed to be there as much as we were ourselves. While we'd known Monica for a bit, we hadn't encountered Susan or Beverly before. They had been friends for many years and were Protestants. We all got on very well (on the banter-in-the-Broadway level); so well that one time, Susan suggested we all go to her house. It was a strange idea to me that anyone's parents, particularly their father, would put up with the intrusion of such a squad. But Susan assured us it would be okay, and it was.

Susan was small – the smallest of all of us – and I think she was also a year younger. She had short dark hair, and even her wee sister was bigger than her. But she was great fun to be around and had a big warm heart. She was kind, very kind.

She had two older sisters who had, in most respects, 'moved on' from the house, and only slept there at night. The front room had been theirs and, although they hardly ever used it now, it still bore their traces: candles, a lot of candles (I think they used to make their own); posters on the walls of everyone from David Essex to Che Guevara; and a big stereo with stacks of records – much better than a jukebox. It was a big room with a high ceiling, plaster centrepiece and even a chandelier. It had a beautiful big bay window looking on to the promenade; a sofa along the back wall; and a number of large pouffes. It had a lovely mahogany table, and an enormous marble fireplace, which was a striking feature. Though it might sound grand, it was cosy. We were welcome there and largely left alone.

Essentially the Smarts' front room was another Broadway – a place for us all to *be*: to be teenagers, play music, have companionship – without the occasional hassle of being put out by Arthur or Lido. I was a bit nervous at the start about Susan's parents and what they would make of us, especially the father. But her mother was absolutely lovely to us, and while Mr Smart would have been a less indulgent person overall, compared to Dad there wasn't a problem. We never had any major issues with either of them, although Mr Smart would tell you to turn the music down if it was too loud. And there was trust, too. Eventually we were allowed to come in and wait for the girls until they turned up.

Throughout 1974 and '75 I would have been there, on average, twice a week. Mainly, but not only, at weekends; and during the day as well as the evenings. For me, and I think for all of us, it grew into something special, unique – something that none of our other friends had. It was like a very special den, our own private club, and we ended up going there much more often than to the youth club. There was a warmth and a comfort. We had great craic, but we could talk too. There was one thing I couldn't talk about, but, really, it was only the one.

The girls were more sensible than us and could make a point in a way you could appreciate and respect – a way you could actually hear and take on board. There was 'sensible craic', if you like, as well as mayhem. That was part of the charm. We could talk about what had happened since the last time we'd met – something at home or school that was maybe on our minds – and there was a sense of an arm being put around you. And although we weren't all from the same background (Mr and Mrs Smart were English), we could talk, without animosity, about the Troubles.

If I mentioned, maybe with bravado, that I was thinking of taking the next step on from NAB, a resounding 'No!' would come back at me with one voice. The girls stopped us; they would talk about how wrong the 'next step' would be, and that they didn't want anything to happen to us. 'Come here instead,' they would say, 'we can do something here.'

We had a very strong bond. That Susan and Beverly were Protestants never bothered me. If anything it was a link, a very rare meeting at the time, with that community. Their kindness and generosity diluted my sectarianism.

The Smarts' front room was a great place to be able to go at that time – which, apart from anything else, was a time when we were transitioning towards adulthood. We were friends first and foremost, and could have conversations. Yes, there were hormones about the place, and we were fairly new to that kind of thing – but while there might have been the odd snog, we were mates first of all. It was like the early days of the TV show *Friends*, before they started going out with each other. Having said that, Dicker and Monica did end up getting married. But towards the end of 'Smarts' Front Room' – from the summer of 1975 – I was going steady with Deirdre.

I'll always treasure that place, and I treasured it at the time. We did, of course, knock about with other people around the town, but we never wanted to jeopardise what we had there by inviting new people along. That group, that gathering, was ours.

We did overstep the mark sometimes, though. Eventually there would have been carry-outs involved – not that we ever wrecked the place or anything – but it could get a bit crazy. For example, every time Seamy Mental came in, he tried to kung-fu kick the chandelier. He could never quite manage it, but one time he got up on one of the pouffes, can in hand, and launched himself at the thing. He went head-over-shite and hit something, which hit something else, and broke one of the fancy bottles that the older sisters cherished. Susan wasn't a bit pleased. We hid the broken glass in the packed straw of a leather (or leatherette) pouffe and zipped it up again. (Years later a friend of ours bought that house, and Dicker was able to warn him about what lay inside that particular pouffe: the remains of the bottle were still there.)

One day in the mid-70s, when the girls weren't around, just me, Dicker and Micky, Dicker introduced us to the wonders of playing with methylated spirits. He lit some of the spirit, and showed us that you could briefly put a finger in the flame without doing serious damage. Me, being me, put two fingers in, then three. And then I took it one step further: I put my penis into the flame. It did burn me slightly, and I've wondered since if there was anything going on there, apart from the bravado. That thing, my penis, had been involved in my abuse. Was I being particularly reckless with the flame for that reason? I don't know.

But I do know that I hold the time spent in the Smarts' front room very high in my heart. It was in that place that I found comfort, companionship and support when God knows I needed those things.

I often wonder now where I might have ended up without it.

Chapter 13

AFTER SCHOOL

I left school in 1975, when I was still just sixteen, and went to catering college. The course was divided between theory and practical, and as part of the latter, I was assigned to the Russell Court Hotel in Belfast. I stayed in Belfast at this time; attended college for the first six weeks, then went to the hotel. I really liked it, but there was a serious lack of prospects. There weren't as many restaurants and bistros then as there are now. There were mainly hotels, and only one head chef in each place. The young chefs would say to us new recruits, 'God, you're mad.' And the hours *were* mad. You lost track of time. When we were in the hotel, we were under their rules, not those of the college; and there were actually occasions when I didn't even know what day it was.

While you were there, you were staff, and you did as they did. You weren't allowed to use the front door, for example. We had to go in via a route that took us under the carpark, and along this subway that led round to the kitchens.

There was an older man who worked in the kitchen washing the pots and pans. He was deaf and had a speech disability, so communicated by pointing at things and gesturing. One day, I was coming in for an afternoon shift just as he was leaving. There were only the two of us in the subway, and as we were about to pass each other he started gesturing at his watch, as if to say, 'You're starting late today. What's wrong with you?' I stopped, but when I did, he put a hand on my shoulder. And put his other hand on my privates.

I ran, and I could see that he was running frantically after me. I remember thinking, 'What is it that people are seeing in me? Do they think that I'm going to be all right with this or something?' I immediately told the head chef what had happened. He was furious, and he called us both into his office the next morning. He gave off in no uncertain terms to the man, who ended up crying. It was made plain to him that if anything like that ever happened again – to me or to anyone else – it would be taken a lot further. I was glad. I felt protected. The head chef had dealt with things – he had, in fact, stopped anything too bad from actually happening – yet I can't honestly say I made any comparison at the time between his behaviour and that of certain church people (Dean Cushenan, for example). Years later, when I was fighting to get justice for what had been done to me, I remember thinking, 'Wouldn't it be great if you could just say one thing to one person and something would be done?', as had happened in the Russell Court. But my main thought back then was, 'What the hell am I giving out here?'

In the end, I decided catering was not for me. Not only were there so few opportunities, but the head-chef system and the gruelling hours were too much. I went home and told Dad, which didn't go down well. He said, 'You needn't think you're just coming back here to sit like a clocking hen,' so I went to see about a trade in the Greenbank Industrial Estate.

I really wanted to do joinery, but I was too late to enrol. Instead I was told there was a painting and decorating course. I knew, from Dad, that sitting on the dole for a while wouldn't be an option, so I signed up.

It was about this time, when I was seventeen, that I had a sniff of fame as a football prodigy. I was playing for Newcastle, and someone from Glentoran had seen me while he was down on holiday. After the match he asked our manager who I was and mentioned that he would like Bob Bishop to have a look at me – Bob Bishop being the scout who had famously discovered George Best.

I went home that night and told Mum and Dad. The story went round the town – and grew in the telling: I wasn't just maybe going for a trial in Belfast, I was going to Manchester United; it was all signed and sealed.

I was even being pointed out from across the street: 'That's him there …'

But if Bob Bishop ever came to look at me, he must have thought, *nah* … Nothing ever came of it.

I did, however, have a trial with Dundalk. Dundalk were the Irish Champions then, and I was brought down for pre-season training and challenge matches. Again it didn't come to anything more, and I went back to playing for Newcastle.

But the significant thing about the Dundalk episode had been Dad. Up to that point he had shown no interest whatsoever in my football. But when the League of Ireland Champions came calling, he couldn't do enough for me. He took me up and down to Dundalk, no questions asked – to Ravensdale and Oriel Park – and he would wait through the training. But when the club's interest in me petered out, so did his own.

By then, my socialising had moved to the Wilmar bar – 'the real thing', if you like. It had a disco, not a jukebox, and it played our sort of music, and on a Friday and Saturday, a group would play. I first started to go with my friends when I was just underage (a couple of them were a bit older than me), and Deirdre was part of the company too sometimes. I enjoyed going there on a Saturday afternoon, sitting with older ones over a bowl of stew and a pint, like an adult.

The alcohol consumed on a night out would quickly scatter what inhibitions I had. It was an easy way of blocking things out if I was ever triggered by anything; if the deeply-buried abuse ever stirred – as it sometimes randomly did – because of a chance remark, the smell of cigarettes, or even a joke. If I was late or had the smell of drink on me at all, Dad would be at the door ready to give me a battering and to give off stink. So I started to get my brothers to leave a window open in our back bedroom, but many's a time he caught me climbing in and put me back out through it. If that happened, I'd just go into the fields behind our estate and try again later. But there were times – as there would be for all of us – when I'd be out all night.

Then came a time when I'd had my fill of all that – of not knowing if the door would be open or locked; of having to go to Mass, and everything else; of being under threat – and I left home. Micky, Dicker and me took off … for Norwich, of all places. We had a friend who was at art college there, and he'd said one time that we should come over. So, in our minds, it was somewhere we knew we'd have a roof and we decided, on a whim, that this was where we were going to head. None of us told our parents, or anyone else. I had reasons – maybe we all had reasons – and we packed our bags. We got the bus down to Belfast, and the ferry over to Liverpool.

When we arrived at Liverpool and came out of the ferry terminal, we hadn't a clue. Do we turn right or left for Norwich? None of us knew. We were pointed in a particular direction and started trying to hitch to Norwich. We passed the Tate & Lyle sugar factory, where there was a wee man in a hut raising the security barrier to let the lorries in and out. We didn't go over to him, he actually came to us. He must have seen these three waifs with their bags and taken pity. He asked us if we were all right, and we told him where we were going. He told us the best route to take – initially in the direction of Derby. Then he said, 'Wait a minute,' and went back into his hut. He brought out a pie – a homemade mince and onion pie, that must have been his lunch – broke it up with his hands and gave it to us. It was just a wee random act, but his kindness meant so much.

We weren't that successful thumbing lifts, and one night we slept in a turnip field. We decided to pool our money and get train tickets as far as they'd take us – with the mighty ruse that, when the conductor came, we'd pretend to be asleep, dodge the ticket inspection, and go even further. It didn't work, and we were ordered off the train.

The next day no one stopped at all. The three of us were struggling, and hungry, and hadn't washed. We must have been a sight. Dicker, being older, and having that bit more sense, peeled off and went to see his big brother in London. Micky and I didn't mind – we felt we might have a better chance of lifts with just the two of us. Sure enough, a van driver did stop for us. He wasn't going to Norwich, but he left us at a town on the route. I can't remember the name, but it was one of those very small places that seems to do well in the FA Cup.

Anyway, we were standing at the side of the road, with our bags at our feet, when a police car passed by on the other side. It stopped, and one of the policemen beckoned us over. He made us leave our bags where they were, and had us get into their car. As we sat in the back seat, they radioed the RUC to try to get some information on us. One of the first things we heard come through the radio was 'known IRA sympathisers'. We looked at each other. There wasn't a mention of NAB.

The word was that we were 'known to local police', but, although there was no mention of us being wanted, the one who had beckoned us over told us to go on to Norwich: 'You're not staying here.' He said that if we didn't move on in short order, we'd be investigated further.

When we got to Norwich, we asked someone on the street where the art college was. I remember my heart sinking when the person replied, 'Which one?' For apparently there was a fabric school, a ceramics place, and on the outskirts, a campus dealing with something else entirely! But the man did say, 'You're Irish. There's a Catholic church over the road.' We rapped the door of the parochial house, not knowing what else to do. If it seems at all odd that I should look for succour from a Catholic church after what had happened to me, I can only say we were desperate. If it had been a Presbyterian church rumoured to help strangers in need, we'd have gone there too. A priest came out, and the very first thing he asked us was if we were Catholics. We were destitute and stuck, but he wanted to know what religion we were! Very hurriedly, he gave us a fiver and told us to move on.

We went into a nearby Wimpy burger bar. I saw our faces in a reflective surface and thought, 'Oh Jesus.' As soon as we'd ordered something to eat, we went into the toilets to clean up.

As it happened, there was a Salvation Army place just across the street. We got a shower and called home from there, and our situation reminded me of a programme I'd seen on TV. 'We're like something from *Johnny Come Home*,' I thought to myself.

The adventure was over. Micky's da transferred money to get us home. When we got into Belfast, I knew what would be waiting for me in Mourne Rise so, instead of taking the bus straight to Newcastle, I got one for Downpatrick. I knew we had a match there that day and it would delay the inevitable. My boots had come over with me, in the bag, to Norwich. I tried to coax Micky but he, rightly, said it was time to go home.

I went to Downpatrick, on my own, and played the match. Dad had to be restrained from coming down and pulling me off the pitch. When I went home, I got everything – a tongue-lashing, as well as a hiding.

Chapter 14

TO LONDON, AND BACK

In November 1977, having gone out with each other since the summer of 1975, Deirdre and I got engaged. Out of all my friends I was the last to have someone serious in my life. I was also the last one to bring a girl home to our house, although I was the eldest. One reason is that I was shy around such things – in fact I hadn't even asked Deirdre out, I'd got Micky to do that – but it wasn't the only factor.

The truth is that I'd steered away from any kind of real intimacy for a long time. As well as the shyness there was something in the back of my mind – because of what had happened to me, obviously – that anything along those lines was 'dangerous' or 'bad'. I went very slowly and carefully. Whereas some friends were seeing this one, that one and then somebody else, that wasn't me. It was only with Deirdre that I formed what you'd call a relationship.

In the spring of 1978 we found out she was pregnant. We were both still very young, and we panicked. We thought that, if we could just get away, get a bit of space, we could sort it out on our own. We left, telling no one.

All of Dad's attitudes – that traditional Catholicism – was part of the reason, no doubt about that. It was that attitude that made us think that we had to leave Ireland altogether. And, even though he was not in the front of my mind – especially with the pregnancy – I have wondered if in a sense I was trying to leave Finegan behind too. But I was nowhere near ready to talk about him, he was still buried deep inside me, and I was taking him with me.

So we headed to London, the biggest city of the biggest neighbour – neither of us having any real conception of what London was like. I knew it was bigger than Belfast or Newry, but just how much bigger than Newry could it be?

Without knowing anyone, without having an address, we landed in London. I had some vague notion that there was an Irish community in north London, so thought we'd try there first. I thought there might be a community there who could help us out, workwise and everything.

We needed somewhere that night, so I lifted the *Evening Standard* and looked at the B&B rather than the agency ads. The first one I saw was in Hornsey, north London. I went over to a phone box and by sheer luck, they had a room. We were there within the hour.

It had been a family home and was divided into rooms. They did cooked breakfasts, mostly for the working men who stayed there – men who had come down from Ireland, England, Scotland and Wales. It was run by a Greek man and his wife, who was the daughter of the house. Her elderly parents still lived in the front part of it. We had a kettle and a wardrobe in our room, and little else. One half of the wardrobe held bread, milk, and stuff for making sandwiches for our dinner. We thought that we could find a place of our own from there. But it was comfortable, and we stayed on – we ended up staying there for the full eight or nine months we were in London.

I wasn't quite finished my apprenticeship back home, but I shimmied round that, and got work as a time-served painter.

The first person I told our news to was my middle brother Brendan. He had his own troubles, with alcohol and with Dad, and was forever heading off on 'adventures'. He was in London with a friend at that time and came over to see us. Brendan's friend had something to eat in our room as I walked with my brother round the block. I told him about the pregnancy, and the first thing he said, in his wisdom, was 'You have to ring home.'

I rang Mum first to the O'Hare's house, where she did a bit of cleaning. There were tears, and relief to hear that we were safe and sound. I didn't hear anything directly from Dad for a long time.

Our daughter Ursula was born on 13 September 1978 and, like any new parents, all our attention turned towards her. The thought of our time there now scares me – we were so young, so far away from home, and with a new baby. But young as we were, we made it work. It wasn't easy, but we intended to stay – even after we'd told our families about the birth. Our main priority was to try and get a house, and we spent our time answering adverts from near and far. Some of the places were pricey, and some were dumps that you wouldn't bring a baby into. We were finding it difficult to get anywhere suitable, so gave ourselves until the end of November, thinking somewhere would turn up. But when December came, and we decided we couldn't spend Christmas there, we headed for home.

Dad's initial reaction to the pregnancy had not been good. I got his anger filtered and second-hand from Mum, and in the end, we were able to have stilted words on the phone. With more time he softened – I think the thought of his first grandchild was a powerful one – and he actually rented a place for us for when we got back to Newcastle. When we landed at the airport, I saw a side of him I'd never seen before. We got out of the plane, apologising to literally everyone, for poor wee Ursula had cried for every minute of the journey. But by the time we walked into the terminal she had stopped. Dad spotted us first, and with an 'Ach, Marie, there she is', this softer man went straight for Ursula, and lifted her out of Deirdre's arms. Then Mum took a turn to hold her, but it was Dad got his hands on the baby first.

At the beginning of 1980, when Deirdre was pregnant with our second child, Gerard, we were still in the flat on Main Street – the one Dad had rented. I hadn't a car then and was working all the hours God sent. When Deirdre went into labour I rang home to Dad for a lift to the hospital, but he said he had loaded his trailer up and couldn't go. I suppose I thought, or hoped, that he'd be prepared to drop everything. What he did do was ring up a friend of his to ask if he would take her. And Deirdre was driven to the hospital in labour by someone she didn't know, which rankled with us both. Gerard was born on 8 February 1980.

But the softer side of Dad I'd seen glimpses of did not disappear completely. When we moved to a bigger home, one with a garden, in Shanslieve Drive, we set up a badminton net for Ursula and ourselves. Deirdre was very good at badminton, and Dad had the name of being a tennis player in his younger day, so when he and Mum came on a visit, those two would have a game. He also had an undeniable soft spot for his grandkids.

On 9 October 1981, Diarmaid was born and we became a family of five. That was also the year we got our own council house, in Burrendale Park Road. It was just round the corner from Mum and Dad's and it was a big moment for us. It was about putting down roots. There was a comfort in that.

And I have happy memories of this time when the kids were very young. We had the house now, I had work, and though we didn't have a car, Micky and his wife Marguerite were very generous with theirs. When they went away for runs and picnics on Sundays, they always included us. We all squeezed into their car, even if it was only a trip of a few miles to Tollymore or Castlewellan Forest Park – the kids loved to roll in the long grass and play in the ponds.

In 1982, when I was working for Morgan and Savage as a painter, Dad came up with an idea. He'd been taking his trailer round the country selling fish, and the place that he always did best was Warrenpoint. He rented a stall in the market there and usually sold out. The next step was to go back to having a shop again – and there seemed no better place to have it than Warrenpoint.

But, of course, with Dad it wasn't a gradual thing. He rented a property straight away, and I did it up for him so he could open. Very quickly, myself and my youngest brother, Declan, were down there giving him a hand. He was busy and started again to do runs out to nursing homes and such like. Instead of leaving it at that level, he took a massive gamble. He got a loan to rip the place out – a place he didn't own – and brought in builders to refashion and refurbish it completely, adding value to a property that wasn't even his. He got new fridges and counters – the best of everything of course. I didn't know the amount he borrowed, and I don't think Mum would have known (that's not how they worked), but from the cut of what he bought, he had borrowed a fierce amount.

On the day the revamped shop opened, he took delivery of not one but two brand new vans, the larger one in the livery of 'The Sea Shell: P Gorman and Sons'. For by this stage – the middle of 1982 – Dad had asked Declan and me to come in with him. The money wasn't good, in fact it was absolutely *un*good, but, as he kept saying, we'd be building this business up for ourselves. He was full of optimism, declaring this was a move he should have made years ago. It was going to be great.

I believed him, or didn't disbelieve him enough, and I gave up my job.

In the beginning, business was good. It was very early starts for me to get to the fish and fruit markets before we opened, and Deirdre didn't appreciate it. I hardly saw the kids. I was home late, tired; and away again before they were up. At the start, me and Declan thought, briefly, that maybe this would take off, but the money was useless – worse than useless – and I was a married man with three children. On a Saturday evening, to supplement the wages, I would fill a box with fish, chicken and vegetables and tell Dad that there were fewer items in it than there actually were. And during the week, if he went out to do a run to the convent, I'd fill another box and stash it until I went home. It doesn't sound great, but I was trying to make ends meet. Without those 'extras', my family would have been in a very bad way indeed.

We had some good times, and some good craic, in that shop. But even when things were going well, the red flags started reappearing. Once again Dad would take to the back of the shop with a couple of men and the racing pages. In no time, they were coming nearly every day. And then the three of them started going to the dog meets in Dundalk. It took me a while, but I realised that history was repeating itself. Once again, we were leaking money to the bookies, and the shop was running on borrowed cash.

The borrowed cash turned out to be borrowed time. The thing that fast-forwarded my thinking to 'I need to get out of this' was one particular day when Dad came back from the bank. He took me to the far end of the shop and said that the bank manager wanted to see me. I could get nothing else out of him; it was as if he had no information except that the manager wanted to see me before he had any more meetings.

I really didn't know what it was about, but I learned very quickly. As soon as I sat down in his office, the manager laid it on the line: 'I don't know if your father has told you,' he said (he hadn't), 'but he's struggling to meet his payments on equipment and vans for the shop.' His suggestion – 'which your father has agreed to' – was, 'If we could transfer half of that borrowing to you, that would ease the pressure from the bank on the business.'

I didn't say this to the manager, but I thought 'What are we even talking about? How the hell could I take on thousands of pounds of debt? I'm taking food from the shop on the quiet just to feed my family!' The long and the short of the thing was I said no.

When I went back to the shop, Dad said eagerly, 'Well what did he say?'

I said, 'Dad you know what he said, and *I* said no.'

Dad hardly ever cursed, but he roared, 'Oh aye. Fuck aye! I'm doing all this for you, for your future, and you won't do this one thing for me. Well, what's the bloody point?'

Very soon after that I knew I had to go. I left in 1985, after not quite three years. And to be fair to him, in the end, I think he saw why. Mum and Dad were living round the corner from the shop by the time I left, and when we were up visiting on a Saturday and I'd call by the shop, there might be only two trays of fish in the window, and some apples inside, still in the box. He could no longer stock the place properly, and I felt sorry for him.

*

Just as I had taken Finegan to London, I brought him back home with me. My buried hurt would surface when I was triggered. And those triggers could be anything – cigarette smoke; the inside of a church … a pair of shoes.

When he was doing things to me, I used to just look down, hang my head. I can remember to this day the shape and style of his shoes. They were very particular, and big – like the rest of him. Back home now, a married man, and out for a walk, I would sometimes bump into an Irish teacher who lived in the town. He'd often ask after our Damian, who was mad for Irish and a former pupil of his, and all I could think of, every time I met him, was how much his big shoes reminded me of Malachy Finegan's.

There's so many things can trigger you, and you don't see them coming.

And if I was triggered during the day, I'd lash out in my sleep at night, and my legs would flail about and waken Deirdre. This was obviously upsetting to her, to be woken by such a disturbance in the middle of the night, and sometimes she would tell me, through tears, 'You were running there.' She didn't know what was going on, and I couldn't tell her.

More frightening, and more hurtful for her, were the times when, in our most intimate moments, I'd see Finegan's face. I'd stop and I'd roar out, and my beautiful young wife would cry. She'd ask me, 'Did I do something or say something wrong?' and I'd say no. A day or two later she'd try to get me to speak, and that led to more rows. I wanted her to stop asking me what was wrong, for I wasn't telling anyone. I just wanted to blend into the sofa, and for the subject to change.

I started going back to the Wilmar in the mid-1980s, but there was something different in me this time – darker, more self-destructive. The buried hurt was really starting to surface. It was shifting inside me; I was losing whatever control I had over it. Maybe just because I had held on to that control too tightly, and for too long. I did what I could to bury it all again, and I drank: serious drinking all the time, drinking with intent. It was all about blotting things out, things that were surfacing more often. That fun element of going to the pub with your friends was more or less gone. This was *consequential* drinking, and my family were suffering the consequences.

Sometimes I'd come home drunk and the kids would be wakened by an argument between me and Deirdre; sometimes they would get up and help put their Dad into bed. And then the following day there'd be my remorse and talk of the promises I'd broken.

The atmosphere was horrible – especially horrible for the kids. It's no excuse, I know, but I was carrying this weight; this weight that no one knew about. And the only thing that lightened the load for me, that seemed able to take me to a different moment, was alcohol.

Around this time, in the autumn of 1986, Mum became very ill. If I'd had the words, and had the strength, she would have been the first person I'd have spoken to about Finegan. Deirdre would obviously have been a very close second, but Mum was the woman who had fought for me not to go back to St Colman's. That wee boy would have talked to his mother before anyone else. But didn't, because he thought she'd had more than enough to contend with in her own life.

Initially the GP, and Mum herself, thought she had gallstones. But very quickly, in September, it was confirmed that she had cancer. The surgeon said, 'There's absolutely nothing we can do. Take her home and be good to her.'

She died at home on 10 December 1986. My sister Moya was great with her, and Dad was kind to her too. Her death left a massive void in me. I didn't handle it very well and, again, my own family suffered. The rails that I'd been wobbling on for my own reasons, I just crashed off completely. I didn't know where to go or what to do. Mum had helped me navigate my way through so much in life. When she died, I just crawled back into my shell. I went back to what I knew – what I knew could blot things out. I was drinking even more frequently now, and to hell with the consequences. Other people suffered alongside me because of my grief.

And I thought, 'Now there's no one I can ever tell my story to.' Mum had, almost literally, been in my corner, for we'd had to fight. When she was gone, I just tried to bury everything again, even deeper. And when I couldn't, when I was triggered, I'd be brought right back into that dormitory again. And my wife and children would be asking questions of a twelve-year-old boy.

Chapter 15

I BELONG TO GLASGOW

For over twenty years, from the middle of the '80s, I regularly went over to Glasgow to support Glasgow Celtic. I joined a supporters' club in Downpatrick that my brother-in-law was involved with. I enjoyed the company of the group of friends I went with, and because we went to the same places all the time, we got to know people there too and made some really good friends.

And Glasgow was another life, in several respects. It was a release valve – offering fewer consequences than the Wilmar. I could come back in a couple of days like I'd hardly been drinking at all: 'Sure look at me, I'm back the way I started when I left.' There was a twelve-hour buffer on the way home to make myself presentable.

But much as Glasgow was a relief, it could also be great fun. We used to stay in a B&B called the Queen's Park, where the breakfast was set down in front of you. It was never enough for two of our number, Big John and Pogo – discreet helpings and wee triangles of toast were of no use to them – so we used to go to a bar that did an all-day breakfast; an 'All

You Can Eat for £3.95' breakfast buffet. They had a canvas banner outside the pub displaying this hostage to fortune.

One day, we were two men down on the bus back for the ferry, and it was suggested that Big John and Pogo might be in the pub. Someone was dispatched to retrieve them and, when he came back, he reported that the head chef – who was replenishing a container of bacon – had cried out, 'Thank fuck! I was about to go out and rip that bloody sign down!'

Another time we were heading back home on a very rough crossing. One minute you'd see the water you were rocking on, and the next minute, sky. Anyone with a drink on the table was hanging on to it for dear life. There were Derry fellas on board with us, anxious to hear word about a Gaelic football match; an important match – an All-Ireland Championship game. Somebody looked out and on the deck, in the gale, was a man holding a transistor radio to his ear. The man nearest the sliding door opened it to find out what the score was.

'Are you listening to the match?' he roared above the waves.

'Yes, I am,' said the other man. 'England are 90 for 3.'

The whole bar erupted.

That core group of us who went all the time got to know local people well, and we'd leave our season tickets with them when we weren't using them ourselves. In return, they'd secure us big game tickets – for cup finals, European matches and so on. We also got to know the owners of the Celtic pubs we went to. Joe Carville owned Hoops, and his uncle (Tommy Carberry) Baird's in the Barrowlands. They treated us well, and Joe used to have a wee area marked 'Reserved' for the Downpatrick ones. He'd have fresh orange and prosecco for us on the morning of a match.

Through Joe, we got to know Celtic players past and present; like Joe Millar, a current star, who became a friend of ours. We also got to meet half of the famous Lisbon Lions, including Bertie Auld, Bobbie Murdoch, and the captain, Billy McNeill.

Another laugh I got was courtesy of David Hay – the former Celtic star who'd come to our house when I was a boy. He'd gone on to have a glittering career and manage Celtic, and the lads always thought I was spoofing when I said he'd been to ours. I saw him after a match one day (he was managing another team), and while he didn't remember the visit in detail, he did recall the fish shop. I asked him if he'd confirm my story, and he said that he would. I presented him to the boys and preened myself, ready for vindication. But Hay began, 'I've never seen this fella before in my life …'

Of such bits of craic and nonsense the Glasgow time was made. And I needed them, every one of them.

Back home, at the end of 1994, the Brendan Smyth case broke, and I was tortured with flashbacks. Chris Moore's UTV *Counterpoint* documentary had exposed him as the paedophile priest he was. Although I wasn't speaking to anybody about it, abuse – clerical abuse – was now a matter of public discourse. Those stories that were starting to surface were my story too. And I was drawn like a magnet to the reportage. If Chris Moore was quoted in six papers after his programme and book came out, I didn't buy one paper to read it – I bought all six. I'd watch the same story four times, on all the different channels. And that story of abuse rolled on. It never seemed to stop.

But the only conversation I was having about it was in my own head. I gathered all this information, but what did I do with it? I took it to the Wilmar with me, or over to Glasgow.

Wives didn't come on the Celtic trips. Occasionally Deirdre would say something like, 'You're not going there again, are you?' or 'Another weekend away, spending money on yourself!' But at the time I just saw that as the sort of exchange that happens between couples.

Glasgow was for me. It was a relief that I grabbed after regularly. Maybe too much.

Chapter 16
LEAVINGS

Newcastle's Burrendale Hotel was, in a way, another sanctuary for me. For over twenty years, from the mid-1980s, I did a lot of work there. The owner, Sean Small, seemed to like me and what I did. Sean, being a builder, was always developing and renovating, and each new upgrade had to be painted and decorated – by me. I grew, as the hotel grew, over the years, you might say. It was brilliant to have such indoor, steady work on my doorstep. It was the work that let me go to Glasgow, I suppose. And I was genuinely fond of everyone I worked with in the Burrendale – from Sean and Jan in the office to Bridget in the laundry. It was the best job I'd ever had, or ever would have; and Dad liked that I worked there.

Dad died on Easter Sunday 1997, also of cancer. Sometimes in a relationship as tense as ours had been, when one party dies it's as if they've let go of their end of a rope – a rope that has stretched taut between them all their lives. Before Dad's final illness I'd honestly say that I'd never had a proper conversation with him in my life. But in that last while, something changed in him, something mellowed. It was a side of him I wished I'd seen more of.

The first real conversation I had with him was in the hospice and we did have a few real talks about things when he was there. Without them, my father would have died a stranger to me. He didn't want to talk about his health – he steered away from that. We would chat about work or the news or the children, his grandchildren. And I remember sometimes leaving the hospice with this warm thought inside me that we'd just had a proper conversation there; man-to-man.

I was there when he died and it was really emotional. The nurses had told us that it 'wouldn't be long now', and in the end it was peaceful. He did try to talk, to say something – I don't know what. But then his breathing just became weaker and weaker, and he slipped away.

I'm sure and certain that I'm still working over the ground of our relationship, but in some ways Brendan's death, in July 2004, hit me even harder.

Brendan was the middle one of the five of us and was probably the gentlest. He had this slightly other-world thing about him, like he was missing a layer of skin. And he drank to a fierce excess from the very start. He was out of the house for weeks at a time as a teenager; was hospitalised for alcoholism when barely out of his teens, and in and out of hospital for the rest of his short life.

All five of us struggled with alcohol, but he was the one carried off by it. Having lived in England for a long time, he spent his last years in sheltered accommodation in Belfast. He was a lovely fella who never harmed anyone but himself.

It was frustrating to watch him let his life slip through his fingers.

I took it really bad. I don't think I told the rest of them just how bad. Damian went to see Brendan a lot, but there were times when I'd be upset with him, and angry – angry because he had so many great qualities and seemed to neither know nor care. It was a call that I knew would come some day, and one I'd been dreading. It was pneumonia and organ failure: he'd given up the ghost.

We waked him in our house, and after the funeral I felt so very guilty. I thought I should have done more, especially as the eldest in the family. I should have been doing what Mum would have done if she'd been there. I thought I'd failed him terribly.

When I first started speaking to doctors and psychiatrists about what was inside me, it was Brendan that I talked about constantly – not abuse. When I did start to talk, it was him on the tip of my tongue. Maybe, in some way, Brendan helped me to get to the other thing. It was very hard to speak about his passing, but it did prove possible. Maybe it would be possible to speak about my abuse.

PART TWO

Chapter 17

LEARNING TO TALK

If you're lucky, the buried thing in you doesn't stay buried forever. The ground shifts, or moves under pressure, and what's hurting you surfaces.

Throughout the 2000s I hadn't been in a great way, and the pressure was building. A real low point came on a day that I was visiting Mum's grave in Warrenpoint. It was in 2003 or 2004, I think, when I passed by a recently erected headstone in the shape of a Celtic cross. It marked the resting place of Malachy Finegan – he had died in 2002.

It stopped me dead in my tracks. The immediate effect was numbing. I would now have to pass Finegan's grave every time I wanted to visit Mum's and Brendan's. Instead, I just stopped visiting; stopped going to Cemetery Sundays.

Later, I felt a pang of regret as I realised that now I would never have a day of reckoning with Finegan. It was one more thing he had taken from me. But there was also some relief that he wasn't in the world anymore and wasn't – could not be – doing what he had done to me to any other boy.

Then, in 2010, the Brendan Smyth case appeared again

– particularly in relation to the behaviour of Cardinal Sean Brady, the Primate, the leading figure in the Catholic Church in Ireland.

The first boy to tell his parents that he'd been abused by Smyth was fourteen-year-old Brendan Boland. In 2010, it became known that, as a young priest, Father Sean Brady had been present as the abused boy was being questioned. It later emerged that the child's father had not been allowed into the room, and Boland had been immediately sworn to secrecy. What Cardinal Brady failed to tell anyone, even in 2010, was that young Boland had given him and his colleagues details of some of the children being abused by Smyth.

While I admired and was inspired by the courage of the adult Brendan Boland in coming forward – courage that I didn't have myself just then – it was all very triggering. It was around that time too that I started to be more aware of photographs of Jarlath Cushenan who, as dean of St Colman's, had clearly seen what was being done to me that day. He was now parish priest of the Hilltown/ Clonduff parish (where Finegan had been before his death). The photos that I saw were of him on happy occasions – First Communions, Confirmations, the retirement of a teacher – and the thing that struck me was that, unlike everyone else, he was never smiling. 'I know why you're not smiling,' I thought, 'you're carrying this too.'

In 2011, I took myself to the GP, Dr Devlin, to talk about 'stress'. It was a difficult thing for me to do. I put it off a few times before I went. It's hard to be precise, but I think that I went to the doctor because I was finding life – and myself –

just too hard to take. Maybe it was to buy myself a bit more time with those around me, I can't be sure.

I didn't say anything too specific to her – just talked about my mood being low, and so on – but she obviously picked up that my mental health was a worrying thing. Without hesitation, Dr Devlin said, 'I'm going to refer you to the hospital.' And I ended up at Downshire hospital – The Mental – the same hospital in which both Brendan and Dad had been patients.

I was under the care of Dr McCleary, and initially assessed by a member of her team. A short time later, I got word of an appointment: Dr McCleary had assigned me to a colleague of hers, Dr Stephen Kelly. Only I knew what had really brought me to this point, but I think it was starting to bubble just under the surface. What I'll always be grateful to Stephen Kelly for is that, in the six weeks or so I was with him, I was able to speak openly, for the first time, about my mental health. He was the one who got me talking, if you like.

When the six weeks ended, he said he'd keep a couple of appointments 'floating' for me and he asked me to phone him when I was ready to continue, 'Because,' he said, 'I think there's something more …'

He was right, but the barrier for me was that he was a man. I didn't fear him or anything like it, but I was thrown back on the problem of trying to find the words. It was going to be difficult to describe what had happened to me and, apart from her experience and being a great psychiatrist, there was something about Dr McCleary that reminded me of Mum.

My next appointment, after I'd finished with Stephen Kelly, was with her. She called me, and held the door open for me to go into her room. I had my back to her as I walked past to take a seat. Before I turned to face her, I blurted out, 'Dr McCleary, I was abused as a child at boarding school.'

That was the first time I heard myself saying those words out loud.

Very quickly, she got me numbers for the specialist sex abuse counselling service, Nexus. She didn't sit me down and say, 'Who was he? … Is he alive? … Is he not?', it was more like a normal appointment after that. But right away, contact was made with Nexus, and with the police.

Deirdre had driven me to the appointment and was waiting in the car outside. I don't know if there was a pale or frightened look on my face, but as soon as I got into the car she said, 'What's wrong?' I think I said something like, 'Drive, just drive.' But before we got home, I told her what I'd just told Dr McCleary. And the first thing she said was, 'Thank God.'

She was thanking God for understanding. For a lot of things made sense to her that hadn't made sense before. It explained at a stroke a lot of my past behaviours, though it didn't excuse them.

I had to go for an initial assessment with Nexus. And it was there that I got official confirmation from the police that Finegan had died in 2002, though I'd already known that, of course.

Although I'd begun to talk about Finegan and what he'd done towards the end of 2011, the release from that pressure cooker wasn't instant. It was a very, very slow thing. But there was a sense of some slight turning in the tide. And I had counsellors now – all of them were women.

But life doesn't happen in straight lines. In late November 2011, before the counselling had the opportunity to have any effect, before it had time to bed in, I had a setback. More than a setback.

I tried to end my own life.

I'm not exactly sure what was in my head. I didn't regret – I have never regretted – beginning to talk about the abuse. But I think it was overwhelming at the start because I'd been silent for so long. And now other people were talking to me about it on a regular basis, and drawing me out; quite rightly, but it caught me off guard. There was a wave of something inside me – and coming at me – that I hadn't anticipated. The wall that had been holding this all back for years had been breached, and there was a fear in me about the roads I'd have to go down.

Looking back now, what I did, I did without really thinking. It came out of a sensation that I needed to get out … right now. I just did it. I didn't leave a note or anything like that.

When I was preparing to do it, getting a spare washing line from the shed, I remember seeing the silhouettes of my grandchildren in my mind's eye – just their shapes. I could see their outlines but couldn't see their faces. Even so I proceeded to attempt to take my own life. I had just begun something; I was ending something now.

But, thankfully, the line broke. And though I had low

points – many low points and thoughts – after that, I never took any steps in that direction again. But it left its mark on me, literally. Before the line broke, it left a weal around my neck. At the time, and for a long time afterwards. I wore a scarf all the time, even in the house.

My family were obviously upset by what I'd done. Though they now knew about my abuse, it had been a bolt from the blue.

They were also distraught when about a month later, on Christmas Day, 2011, in another spur-of-the-moment thing, I completely shaved my head. Christmas has always been a difficult time for me, because some of the most horrific acts of abuse (they were all horrific) had occurred just before the Christmas break, and after I'd come back.

We were all at home. Everyone had gathered for the Christmas dinner, and I went out to the shed and shaved my head into the sink. Our ones used to joke that, if we were going out anywhere, I would take more time with my hair than their mother would. And there I was coming into the house on Christmas Day like a plucked bird. They all burst into tears when I came back in. That incident struck at the hearts of them.

I brought what had happened, and everything else, into the counselling.

I received counselling under the auspices of two separate bodies – Nexus and Towards Healing. Nexus is a specialist organisation dealing with all sorts of sex abuse; and

Towards Healing is a body funded by the Catholic Church to specifically help victims of clerical abuse. Without any admission of liability, the Church paid for my sessions there as soon as I came forward. I would say that this was the very least they could do.

Towards Healing began its work in 2011, and in its first year provided 28,000 face-to-face counselling sessions and answered 12,000 calls to its helpline. Although funded by the Catholic Church in response to emerging abuse research, such as the devastating 'Ryan Report' of 2009, its counselling was completely independent. (I can attest to its independence as someone who has very little faith left, but who has received important, life-saving counselling there.)

There was some overlap between the Nexus and Towards Healing sessions. Nexus sessions began in a clinic in Downpatrick with a woman called Helen Clarke, who was great with me. We had, very cautiously, continued the conversation about abuse, and then I started to go to Belfast as well, and – as part of the Nexus process – took part in a group.

There were a dozen of us, and I was dubious and nervous at the start. In fact, some of them told me later that, after the first meeting, they were sure I was the one in the company who would never be back. But very quickly I realised I was in a room with fantastic people. We got a lot from each other, as well as from Donna, the counsellor. They just *got* me – we got each other. And I found they made suggestions, rather than told me things: 'I know exactly what you mean, Gerard, and when I'm like that, I find that this helps …'

Sometimes, in the days between group meetings, a certain feeling or situation would come up, and I remembered what someone had said, and it steered me round that obstacle. The people in that group were some of the best counsellors I ever met on my journey.

Another thing that helped me was a reconnection with art. You'll have gathered that I wasn't the most studious scholar who ever emerged from St Louis, but I did like art. I liked it, and I was good at it. I remember one report card I got that was littered with lowly letters, and my single A for art. The form teacher's comment said drily, 'Consistent, with glaring exception …'

At one of my appointments, Dr McCleary mentioned that there was a day hospital where people who'd been struggling with their mental health did arts and crafts. Some people found it of great benefit, and she wondered if I would be interested. She walked me over to Finneston House herself to have a look. I had a word with Rosie, the psychiatric nurse, and Margaret, her auxiliary (who was brilliant). I said nervously that I'd come to the next session myself.

Rosie wasn't a trained artist or anything, she just saw the value of art as a way of helping people. It was great for me. I could get lost in what I was doing. And in the casual chats with people – we had coffee and biscuits and all sorts – there was great benefit too. Having not done anything since school, I was drawing and painting again. We also went to the beach and collected dried wood and pebbles, and did pebble art. We all got so good that we started to have sales of our work, and whatever we raised was ploughed back in for art materials. It became something of a cottage industry.

Later on, my artwork would be used by bodies such as SAVIA (Survivors And Victims of Institutional Abuse), but while that was very gratifying for me, personally, it was not as important as the other things the art sessions gave me. Some of the best laughs I've had in my life were in that day hospital, or in the room where the Nexus group convened in Belfast.

One thing that I would say to people with buried hurts, who guard them as if they were precious cargo, is that there are good people out there – people who will help you. I've met so many good people myself – people searching for help and for peace; and those counsellors and others who are willing and able to help them. The important thing is to get to a point where you are able to say what's wrong.

It was because I finally spoke out that I got to meet Hazel and Roisin, my counsellors at Towards Healing, and Hazel was with me for so many steps on the long road. At the time of writing, Roisin still is.

There was some overlap, as I said, with Nexus, but after about twenty-six sessions with them, my counselling continued, and did for a long time, with Hazel. Quite early on she made me aware of the upcoming Hart Inquiry, a public inquiry into historical abuse at Northern Irish institutions. She thought, as I did, that this would be a way for me to take the next step: by giving evidence to that inquiry or making a submission to it. We both thought the terms of reference would include boarding schools – nothing if not institutions

– and I made contact with the Hart team, giving them an outline of what had happened to me.

The letter I got back said that they'd be in contact nearer the time, and that anything I told them would be treated as confidential. It was a spare enough response, but it was heartening. I felt I was getting somewhere. And then, at the end of November 2012, I got another letter to say that boarding schools had been specifically excluded from the Hart remit:

I am afraid this means the inquiry will not be able to consider your application, and so will take no further action in relation to it.

For me it was a plunge of the rollercoaster. I'd built myself up; imagined myself standing shoulder-to-shoulder with other people who had been abused and telling my story. So to be told that, sorry, our terms of reference don't include you, was devastating.

But Hazel's response was, 'Don't let the bastard get away with this' – or she might have said bastards, I honestly can't remember. Either way, she urged me to take a civil case – which for me would mean holding both Finegan and the Church to account.

Hazel realised that the wee boy inside me needed hearing. Which is exactly why I embarked on the case ... and why I am doing this book.

*

I didn't exactly know what 'taking a civil case' meant. Initially I was just looking for advice, and my brother Damian knew a lawyer, Claire McKeegan, who was a great friend of his daughter. She has her own firm now, Phoenix Law, but at the time she was working for KRW Law, Kevin Winters' human rights firm.

My first conversation with Claire was very informal – just a conversation with someone friendly who could give me pointers. I told her what had been done to me, where I was, and that I was stuck. I was stuck because the Hart Inquiry had got my hopes up, and then let them down. I asked her what proceeding with a civil case might entail. I said I wanted to find out how what had happened to me had been allowed to happen. And I wondered if the fact that Finegan was dead would mean that there was no case to answer for anyone else.

But Claire said absolutely not, and she encouraged me. She said that I should take it further, and I made an appointment to go to her office – to tell her my story again, 'officially', so to speak. At that early stage, what I wanted was for Finegan to be exposed. I felt that the wee boy I had been might be stepping from the darkness, and I needed him to be heard and be believed.

I also needed to be taken by the hand through the legal maze.

One day I was in the office talking with Claire – this was an official case now – when Kevin Winters came in and introduced himself. Claire did all the heavy lifting on my case, but he said he wanted me to know that his ears had pricked up as soon as he'd been made aware of my details. For he had gone to St Colman's himself and knew only too well the type of character Finegan had been. He said he realised, looking back, that Finegan had tried to groom him too. 'I didn't suffer anything like you did,' he said, 'but I know, personally, the type of man we're talking about, and we're going to help you in every way that we can.' (Writing in the *Irish News* in December 2021, Winters said publicly that he had been groomed and gave his opinion that 'Finegan was operating his own industrial grooming system. It remains a scandal today that no one in authority was able to step forward and say they knew what was happening or acknowledge having any suspicions.')

Since the Hart Inquiry disappointment I had felt that, apart from my family and counsellors, I was alone with this thing. But here were Kevin and Claire both saying that they believed me. This was crucial encouragement at an early, critical stage.

Once mine was an official case, I had to meet with the police. Even though it was a civil case, and we all knew Finegan was dead, I had to sit down with them and go through my story in a formal interview. They asked me to go to a police station to do this, but Hazel's offices happened to be near the police station in Banbridge and she suggested that they might come to me and do it there.

John Nelson was the policeman who came to see me, and I'm glad to say he was obviously well trained in that kind of interviewing. He was sympathetic, which was good for me, because I had to go into deep detail again, 'for the record', as it were. I was grateful that this could take place somewhere that I was comfortable and familiar with. And after the first interview had run for a certain time, Hazel was able to say, 'I think that's enough for today,' and that was all right. Nelson immediately agreed, and said he'd come back as often as it took.

Things were happening, but at a pace I didn't always understand: the pace that they had to; a snail's pace; the pace of the law.

Chapter 18

LEAVING WORK
AND LEAVING HOME

A big part of your identity, if you're lucky enough to have a job, is the identity that comes from your work and how you do it. I think it's fair to say that I had a good name as a painter and decorator. I had a bit of a reputation for delicate or 'tricky' work and Sean and Jan from the Burrendale recommended me to many of their friends – people who, like themselves, had beautiful houses.

But since Brendan's death in 2004, there had been periods in which I was unable to work due to problems with my mental health. The shutter wouldn't fall all at once; I'd have dips, take a break from a job, and then go back to it. But when the full impact of having to deal with the abuse kicked in, my mood, and my ability to work, was further compromised. Because I worked on my own, and not on building sites, what I did was very much one-to-one and personal. But when I had a bad dip, I just couldn't deal with anyone. There were times when I had to walk off jobs to gather myself.

There were things I was normally confident about – things

like papering a ceiling – that not every painter and decorator would be happy to do. But I found I was maybe dropping paste or knocking things over. There was a gradual erosion, rather than a sudden collapse, of my confidence. The thing that I was starting to process in my head was moving faster than the cogs could take. By the time I first mentioned my abuse to Dr McCleary I wasn't working at all. And I haven't been able to since.

I couldn't work, but not working did my sense of self no good. My world was getting smaller and smaller as it was – my family and counsellors were worried about how isolated I was becoming. They wanted me to get back into society and some sort of normal routine, but they might as well have been telling me to climb Everest.

I didn't cut myself off from outside contact completely, though. Dicker had died in 2011, which was another difficult thing to deal with, but through all of this I kept in touch with Micky. He was a great support, just to sit with, as someone outside of the family. Though he knew by that stage what had happened to me, I didn't always have to discuss 'my abuse case' with him. That, in itself, would release a bit of pressure.

Despite that, all I really wanted to do was to just sit by myself within my own four walls.

In August 2014, I moved out of the family home in Burrendale Park Road and into a flat of my own in Causeway Road – just across from the Broadway Cafe. Back at home there had been times when my head felt as if it was bursting. I know I wasn't the easiest person to live with and thought that my family had suffered enough. They would have preferred that I'd stayed, but for myself, and in my own head, I had to leave. I felt that when I was down, I was dragging everyone down. And I thought that in my own place if I was having a bad day I could have it on my own. I knew, most times, what I could be doing and should be doing, but there were times when all I wanted to do was nothing at all. I felt that, if I put some distance between me and my family, it might help everybody.

Deirdre and the children might not have wanted me to leave but, as always, they supported me – through tears sometimes – and they said, 'If you think this is going to bring you some peace, go ahead and do it.' We still spoke after I'd moved, we speak to this day, and they have all continued to help me in any way that they can.

There is a tremendous ripple effect from abuse which not everyone – and especially the Catholic Church – seems to understand. The ripples are deep and wide, and their effects can be devastating. My family had suffered, just as I had, and they wanted closure too.

I could try to describe the effects that the abuse I suffered had on Deirdre, Ursula, Gerard and Diarmaid, but my words would fall short. Instead I want to let them speak.

Later on, towards the end of my case, each of them had to make 'impact statements', and the final paragraphs of these are reproduced here. Their voices deserve to be heard too:

To say that Malachy Finegan ruined my husband's life is a major understatement. That person took away my husband's innocence, abused his position and left him with a lifetime of guilt which did not belong to him. He took the light out of my husband's eyes and left them empty and dead. He stole my marriage and the man that I love and left my children with the shell of a person he was for many years. ... I was brought up a Catholic, and he has also stolen my faith.

Deirdre

When that priest abused his position of power, abused the trust of his pupils, and subjected my dad to horrific emotional and sexual abuse, not only did he take away his childhood, but his selfish actions had a powerful and profound impact on Dad's capacity to be a loving parent. A devastating impact that we have had to endure and manage on a daily basis, and that WE ALL have to live with for the rest of our lives. That priest has destroyed the quality of Dad's life, and invariably ours too.

Ursula

I am a father to a wonderful, amazing daughter who doesn't know her grandad the way I do. She has never had the chance to see him full of life and fun. As a family, we have been robbed of the life we all deserve: my dad has had his happiness stolen in the most appalling and distressing way imaginable; I have lost my dad and my friend; my mum has lost her husband. My dad has been robbed of the joy of seeing his children become loving parents, and nothing will ever bring that back. The years my dad has suffered in silence have had a devastating impact on our family. We all carry the burden and the guilt of years of sadness.

Gerard

The vile actions of the 'person' who did this to my dad have had a profound and lifelong impact on my dad, his emotions, his mental health and general well-being, and also a lasting effect on the rest of the family. I say again, my father always has been, and remains, a good man who would give anything for his family. But he has been robbed of his innocence, his childhood, and his ability to deal with things and process the emotions that a normal father and husband has. The increasingly apparent fact that this could all have been prevented if only the people in authority who knew of this priest's vile behaviours had acted appropriately and with humanity and with the best interests of their congregations rather than their positions, makes all of the effects of the vile abuse my father endured all the more difficult to accept and live with.

Diarmaid

Chapter 19

OBFUSCATION AND DELAY

When the civil case finally started moving, I found the pace hurtfully slow. And I'd lay the blame for that – and the fact the case dragged on for years – firmly at the doors of the Diocese of Dromore, the Catholic Church and its lawyers.

From the very beginning the omens were not a bit good. First contact with 'the other side' came when Claire contacted the lawyers for Dromore, the diocese in which St Colman's is located, and asked for 'disclosure' on Finegan. In the early stages of the litigation process, each party has to disclose any documents or other information that would reasonably be considered relevant to the case going to court, but from the very start of my case, it seemed like disclosure was more about *non*-disclosure. I wanted to know who had known about Finegan. When did they know? And why didn't they stop him? But the word came back that they had nothing to disclose, which I took to mean, 'He has never come to our attention.'

I can only tell you how it felt, and it felt like Claire had to pull teeth: she had to write to the diocesan lawyers three or four times for the same bit of information; documents would arrive with one or two pages missing; things were given only when they could no longer be held back. This was my experience for the next five years. The particulars – the specific documents or information being sought at a given time – have become blended and blurred together, yet one key thing remains with me: it never felt like 'the other side' was trying to help.

I'm not stupid; I know that their legal team had a job to do for the diocese, and I appreciated that there might be an adversarial element to the case. But this was a church, the Catholic Church, we were talking about and even though, by this stage, I had lost not only much of my personal faith, but almost all faith in the bona fides of the Church, I still had a small remaining hope that they were about what they *said* they were about – looking after people, especially the sheep of their flock. Yet I can honestly say that in the five long years of my legal case, they never gave anything they didn't have to. Not one thing; not once.

It felt to me, as someone with no legal background, that their lawyers were playing a long, hard game. There would be delays, faffing about, quibbles and what seemed to me like deliberate misunderstandings. Things that should have taken days took weeks, and things that should have taken weeks took months (at least). It would have been farcical if it hadn't been painful. One time I was even asked to provide proof that my father had actually sent me to the school:

The First Named Defendant is unable to admit or deny that the Plaintiff was placed by his father as a pupil at the school in or around 1971, and requires the Plaintiff to prove same ...

As Claire began to obtain pertinent documents and information from the diocese, I felt like saying to their lawyers, 'Was that so hard for you? Because it *was* hard on me.' But so often there was swerving – obfuscation and delay. And there was one delay in particular that caused me considerable anxiety.

As part of my case I had an independent assessment done by a psychiatrist in Belfast. The 'other side' said, 'Thank you for doing that, but we use our own,' which meant I was going to have to go through the whole thing again, from scratch. And the thought of that wasn't easy. A psychiatrist wants to know *everything*: how you were abused; where you were abused; in what part of you were you abused. From having been silent for forty years, I was now having to tell my story so often, and to strangers, to men – 'Could you just go over that bit again?' And again, and again ...

In any case, I steeled myself to go to Dublin to meet their appointed psychiatrist, but the wait for the appointment lasted for weeks, which turned into months, then months into many more months. The waiting turned something septic inside me, and in desperation – and for the sake of my own well-being – I decided to reach out and try to do something about it. I decided to appeal directly to the Catholic Church.

Now, obviously, you can't get through to the head of the hierarchy straight away. But I got through to someone who, as well as being a significant link in the chain, had a special responsibility for safeguarding and child protection. I told her that what I wanted was straightforward: to hasten the process of seeing 'their' psychiatrist, to lessen my pain. For my head was fried with the prospect of another 'fresh' session in Dublin – a session that didn't seem to be happening, and that was holding everything up. I appealed to her compassion and asked her on a human level – parking the legalities and everything – could she find out, through the Bishop and his legal representatives, why this was taking so long?

After talking to me on the phone, she came down to see me at the flat. She asked me if I wanted to go through what had happened with her, but I said no. That this was about a very specific thing: the hold-up. Was it necessary? Was it useful? Was it just?

She was pleasant enough with me – I can't say I had a terrible time in her company – but the next day I got word back that 'because of data protection' my case could not be discussed. I had reached out for help, directly to the Church, and that was the response.

It wasn't the only response: she sent me something through the post which, though it wasn't intended to, annoyed me greatly. She said that, understandably, I might have lost contact with the Church and with God, but that I might like to 'avail of the Towards Peace programme (leaflets enclosed)'. Now, I had suffered horrifically – I had been raped, at the hands of a priest – yet she'd sent me a leaflet that told me, 'This service is for those whose faith has been damaged by abuse … [events are] run by women and men – lay and religious – and priests.'

No harm was meant, but could they not see the insensitivity? I was pleading for help on a very particular matter, and the response was, we can't help you with that – but what about getting in touch with God again, and *with priests*?

They just didn't get it. They're just not getting it still.

And I wasn't the only one who experienced their callous lack of empathy. In the Towards Healing group meetings I started going to in Dublin I made a connection with a man called Jimmy. The priest who had abused him and others in the parish had been jailed, but years later Jimmy got notification from the Guards that he was getting released. On hearing that, Jimmy went to the parochial house and told the parish priest that he assumed the man would not be returning to the district, because of the pain he had caused so many people there. But the priest let him know that he wouldn't be right to assume that, because the man was entitled to 'come home', as it were. My friend reiterated his point about the suffering he'd been caused, only to be told by the priest, 'But, Jimmy, *he's* suffering too …'

Jimmy was a big man, and he told me that, in that moment, he was very glad he'd just completed an anger management course: 'I never was so close to reaching across a table in my life …'

The obfuscation and delay on their part caused a lot of

frustration on ours. It seemed that, in travelling from A to B, we often had to go through C, D and E before we got there. Although some of that was probably inevitable, part and parcel of legal cases, it was alien to me. The Church's behaviour, manifested through its lawyers, would have one thought going round in my head: 'Is this what the God you serve would expect from you?' Their actions seemed only to be about limiting damage to the Church's reputation, and in my naivety, I had expected better than that. There's a very concrete example of this in a 2011 exchange of letters I've seen between three very senior Church people: the then Bishop of Dromore, John McAreavey; Cardinal Marc Ouellet, Prefect of the College of Bishops in Rome; and the Archbishop Emeritus of Westminster, Cardinal Cormac Murphy-O'Connor. The exchange concerns an anonymous letter the Bishop had received in relation to Finegan. And while in a letter to Cardinal Oullet McAreavey does include a promise to take positive action to address the issue, his response to the anonymous letter is telling:

> I called a meeting with my solicitor, my media advisor and the diocesan designated person for safeguarding. We agreed to prepare a holding statement that could be used in the event of queries about this situation …

In a short reply, Cardinal Murphy-O'Connor comments, 'Of course I agree that anonymous letters cannot be taken too seriously …'

I have seen many letters, and I have had many

conversations, in which it is crystal clear that victims of clerical abuse are not being taken seriously enough. And that is a pain as real as any physical pain.

My own mental health suffered terribly. In the five long years of my case, I was close to giving up a lot of times. If I hadn't had such support around me, I don't know how I might have ended up. I felt that the Church and its lawyers were an elephant on the road in front of me, and – despite my own lawyers being so proficient, and so profoundly on my side – that elephant wasn't moving. A voice inside me said, 'What did I tell you? What did you expect?'

One of the things that really helped at the time was the company of Cassie, my Bernese Mountain Dog. We used to go to the hills together, and all these things I'm telling you, I told her too. We'd sit at the quarry, or beneath the old television mast that sits above a clearing to the right of the Glen river, and we'd look down at the town. She was a great companion, and she was a reason to get up and out in the morning. I don't know that I would have bothered on my own.

Apart from Cassie, there was my family (of course), and Hazel and Claire keeping me going. And very importantly, a voice that was becoming increasingly significant: that of my twelve-year-old self, saying, 'Keep going, Gerard. I've stepped out of that room now. Don't let me down.'

Chapter 20

A SETTLEMENT (OF SORTS)

In the middle of 2017, I caught sight, for the first time, of my day in court. But, like a series of mirages, dates kept disappearing on me. A key witness would be unavailable; another taken ill. And there was the usual slew of slow business to be done: 'interrogatories' to be formally put and answered; impact statements taken; and medical reports supplied (my appointment with 'the other side's' psychiatrist in Dublin had eventually taken place ... after more than a full year of waiting). And although there were barristers involved now – and in that sense the whole thing had moved up a gear – it seemed to have stalled.

It took the involvement of Ian Elliott, a child safeguarding consultant, to get things moving again.

It was Claire's idea to involve Ian, and it was a good one. He is an authority in his field and has worked all over the world. In fact, from 2007 to 2013 he was CEO of the National Board for Safeguarding Children in the Catholic Church in Ireland. So he was known to them, and he knew about them. He told us that senior Church people could have 'secret files' – files that could only be accessed if you requested them specifically – and he mentioned 'the doctrine of mental reservation', a defence used by the Church for centuries as a way to justify not telling the truth; whether through a 'lie of necessity' or by choosing to answer questions in as limited a way as possible. This, to me, was a real beauty. In essence, it meant the Church's stance was, 'We can do lesser evil to prevent another being done.' With this approach senior prelates could choose to only answer the very specific, literal questions put to them rather than the thing they knew – and that everyone knew – was really being asked. In this way they might 'reserve' information 'for the good of the Church'. That's certainly an attitude I'd experienced in the course of my case.

As soon as it became known Ian Elliott was on board, the pace of everything seemed to pick up. Responses from the other side certainly came faster.

A preliminary hearing was arranged for October 2017 in the High Court in Belfast, and the date arranged was kept this time. On the day, their lawyers and our lawyers were in the same building, in separate rooms. Ian Elliott was there, as was I, and I kept my family posted on the phone. There was a lot of toing and froing between the two rooms and, to be honest, it seemed a bit crude to me. I am trying to avoid the term 'horse-trading', but you get the idea.

A date was set for a full hearing in a couple of weeks, but at one point one of my barristers said, 'In an ideal situation, Gerard, what would it take for this to end here today?'

I said, 'Do you realise how that sounds to someone like me?' For instantly I was triggered: 'Here's sweets; here's a

Dymo printer – take these and go away.'

They said that they had intended nothing of the sort and were only relaying messages from the other side. They explained that the reason we were there that day for a preliminary hearing was to see if we could avoid going to court, 'Which would be difficult for you too, Gerard.' I had previously been told that the lead barrister engaged by the diocese could give me a hard time, and I remember thinking, 'Why? Why would he do that? Why would *they*?'

For me, it was never about money. At the top of my personal priorities was the removal of Finegan's headstone. It was impossible to go to visit Mum's grave without passing his, so I told my barristers that I wanted his Celtic cross headstone removed. But they said that, if the case did go to court, no judge would want to be involved with the like of that. There would be so many other people's sensitivities involved. I asked them if they were asking for my list or telling me what could and couldn't be on it.

Even now, I don't like to think about this in terms of a 'wish list' but the next most important thing to me was acknowledgement from someone senior in the Church – an acknowledgement and apology over the harm that had been done to me. If I wasn't going to have my day in court – a day when I could look John Cushenan in the eye and ask what he did and didn't do, having seen me abused – I wanted someone to say, openly, 'We know that this happened to you.' I also thought that I might like to visit the school … well, not 'like' exactly, but I thought that it was something I might benefit from. A fella called Liam from the Dublin group had said that he'd revisited a home he was abused in as a child and felt that he'd been able to 'rescue' the wee boy he'd been from the building. That idea stayed with me, and I thought I might try it myself.

I made it clear all along that the one thing I would never accept was a non-disclosure element to any agreement. Since it had taken me so long to open my mouth, no one, least of all the Church, was going to tell me to shut it. I also made it clear that, while I understood money was part of the discussion, it was bottom of my personal agenda; it meant nothing to me.

One of the barristers wrote these things down, which was bizarre to me. But what was really surreal was the back-and-forth that occurred: I was sitting in a room with Claire, while a group of barristers representing me (who I'd only met recently) were off in a room talking about me with ones I'd never met.

It seemed, at least among the barristers, that most of the things I was asking for wouldn't be a problem – with the exception of the headstone. But my side assured me they'd pursue that with serious purpose, because of the hurt it caused me. They asked me then if we had an agreement, and at that point the twelve-year-old took over and spoke for me … spoke out loud for the first time in forty-seven years. He said, 'I'll think about it.'

If you like, there *was* a settlement that day, but I hadn't agreed to it yet. I think my barristers were taken aback, surprised. I could see them saying, 'Oh …'

A few days later, Kevin Winters himself phoned me

and, having discussed it with my family, I said yes to the agreement.

Not long after the settlement, I received a letter via my solicitor which purported to be the acknowledgement of harm from the Church. It had been sent by the Most Reverend John McAreavey, the then Bishop of the Diocese of Dromore, and, as far as letters of acknowledgement go, it fell very far short. It talked about how 'school years should be a happy time', and 'the trauma you describe'; of how he had been 'fully informed about the progress in your case,' and so on. If I had hoped for a heartfelt, vulnerable acceptance of wrong done, I'd been crazy. And to cap it all, the letter hadn't even been signed by him; it had been stamped.

This made me feel that all the words the Church was saying publicly – about how this was a new dawn in its treatment of abuse victims – were just that: words. Whereas this was evidence of carelessness and of a lack of respect.

I had a meeting with McAreavey on 28 November 2017 in the parish centre opposite Newry Cathedral. This meeting had been another part of the settlement. Deirdre came with me. (My sons had also wanted to attend, but we got word from the other side that they didn't know there was a 'posse' involved, so in the end, they couldn't go.) We were brought through to the room at the back set aside for the meeting. McAreavey came in, and there were the usual formalities: did we want tea or coffee or anything? We wanted nothing.

Hazel, my counsellor, had suggested that I should write

126

down the things I wanted to ask – What was known about what Finegan did? How did he get away with it for so long? Why was the Church so secretive and difficult in its dealings with people like me? – but when I opened my mouth to speak, not a word would come out. I cried for the rest of the ninety-minute meeting, without saying one single thing. He went out to get me tissues, and that's where Deirdre took over.

She had no files, nothing, but was as good as any barrister would have been. She had done her homework and had everything at her fingertips. She asked blatant, searching questions: when he was based in Maynooth, and advising others about Finegan, why had he never advised them to report him to the police? He was very uncomfortable. He tried to change the subject and shuffled in his chair when Deirdre asked him direct questions about what he'd known, and what he'd suspected. He did say a few things he mightn't have said in court – that he didn't like Finegan, for example, and found him a bully – but Deirdre wasn't to be deflected. She told McAreavey, 'You're the bishop now, sitting here in front of us, and you did nothing.' I was the boy in the roomful of adults that day.

She brought up the letter of acknowledgement – how inadequate it had been; how passive its tone – and pointed out, in a straightforward way, that he hadn't even deigned to sign it. The following morning, a much more humane, signed letter arrived. McAreavey delivered it by hand. To be honest, my family were pissed off by the Church's behaviour at this stage, but I felt a quiet sense of achievement that this had, eventually, been done right. I felt it for the twelve-year-old boy.

A few months later, I would learn that McAreavey had celebrated Finegan's funeral Mass.

Things happened quickly, maybe a little too quickly, at that time. After years of nothing, a painful nothing, there was one development after another. The headstone was taken down in December 2017 (that happened very quickly), and very little now marked where Finegan lay. I felt able to visit Mum and Brendan's grave again.

The next thing was my visit to St Colman's, a few weeks later.

Again, members of my family wanted to come with me for support, but I didn't want to run the risk of being an unintended tour guide: 'There's where we used to study; here used to be the refectory.' I wanted to go straight to the storeroom, my safe place, my sanctuary. I wanted to sit there for ten minutes, talk to the child, and assure him he wouldn't be hurt any more. Then I wanted to go to the dormitory and take that twelve-year-old with me when I left the building.

That was the plan, but it didn't work out like that.

The visit had been arranged for a time when the school wasn't full of children. When I pulled up, I was very nervous, but the principal, Cormac McKinney, was good with me. In fact, I knew him already as he had taught my three children in St Louis – the convent school I'd gone to myself. We went into a main corridor and it was exactly as it had been on the day my father left me off, which was disconcerting. As was the fact that the safeguarding woman – the one I felt had let me down – was waiting inside the school. Mr McKinney asked me where I wanted to go, and I told him. The two of us headed towards the stairs. But as we went up, my left leg started to spasm and, try as I might, I couldn't bring it under control. We came back down the stairs and I said I needed to get some air. He told me to take my time – whatever time I needed.

When I came back in, he suggested that I try the other staircase. But I didn't get more than one step up that staircase before I had visions of Malachy Finegan coming down it. And then I saw a photo of the late Bishop Brooks on a wall: Francis Gerard Brooks, who'd been a teacher in my time. Brooks, who'd been a friend of Finegan's; who had gone on holiday with him; had taken his part; and done nothing about him. As a result of my case, the Board of Governors of St Colman's – whose chairman was Bishop McAreavey – had, in late 2017, instructed that any photographs of Finegan be removed from display in the College, but why was a photograph of Brooks still hanging there?

I wanted to leave but, before I did, I glanced up and caught a glimpse of the storeroom. I came back out and said to Mr McKinney, 'I'm sorry for wasting your time but I can't do this today, I can't do it now.' I went into the car and cried hard for a full ten minutes.

I haven't returned to the school since.

I'm not sure I ever will.

Chapter 21

'BURIED SECRETS'

So while there was a settlement at the end of 2017, not everything had been settled within me. One of the things that rankled most was that Finegan had not been named publicly. He had certainly not been 'named and shamed' by the Church. I mentioned this to Claire, and she had a word with a team from the current affairs television programme *Spotlight* as they had been in with her on another matter. With my permission, she told them about me.

I was put in touch directly with reporter Mandy McAuley and producer Denise O'Connor, and within a short time, they came to film me in my flat. Claire was in the room too, and my brother Damian was sitting beside me, just out of shot, as I told my story.

Mandy and Denise dug deep – not only with me, but around the whole Finegan case. They discovered senior figures in the Catholic Church had known about him and had often discussed him while he was still alive. It was they who found out, for the programme, that McAreavey had invited him to concelebrate a special Mass organised to mark 150 years of the Hilltown/Clonduff parish and that McAreavey had been the celebrant at Finegan's funeral.

The *Spotlight* team contacted McAreavey for a statement a few weeks before the show aired (on 14 February 2018) and it was only then, in a statement to both *Spotlight* and to the wider media, that he publicly acknowledged that he 'first became aware of allegations of child sex abuse against Fr Malachy Finegan in 1994' when he, McAreavey, provided pastoral support to a victim and his family.

In 1994, because of Chris Moore's work, the whole of Ireland was alert to the issue of clerical abuse and, according to McAreavey, 'it was the practice of Bishop Brooks [the then Bishop of Dromore] to report allegations to the civil authorities' and that 'in 1995 the then bishop and his legal team were aware that they had a responsibility to report this particular allegation of abuse'. He did not, however, say if the abuse had been reported in 1995. In fact, the programme reports that, at the time, McAreavey expressed concerns that Brooks had failed to act. It's now generally accepted that Church authorities had known about Finegan much earlier than that, but, according to the *Irish Times* (though this is disputed), it was 2006 before the Church reported any allegation about him to the police.

Within a month of the broadcast of the *Spotlight* episode, 'Buried Secrets', John McAreavey had resigned as bishop because of the intense media scrutiny.

Spotlight revealed that, in the week after McAreavey's public statement, fifteen more of Finegan's victims contacted the programme, and intimated that the true number was likely to be in double, if not triple figures. They interviewed two other men, Paul Gilmore and Sean Faloon, who'd been abused by Finegan while young – Faloon since 1989, when he'd been ten, and an altar boy in the Hilltown/Clonduff parish where Finegan was parish priest.

Following the accusation against Finegan in 1994, Bishop Brooks (a friend of Finegan's), sent him to Our Lady of Victory Trust, a centre run by the Servants of the Paraclete in Stroud, Gloucestershire, for the treatment of priests with a range of different problems, from alcohol and drugs misuse to serious sexual misconduct.

Finegan didn't want to go. I have seen his assessment interviews from December 1994, and they contain comments like:

> His lack of awareness regarding the seriousness and far-reaching consequences for the victims, for himself, and the Church is apparent ... From my conversations with Fr Finegan I think one of his main concerns isn't actually the victims, but the possible effects on his own family of revelations in the press of what actually happened.

Finegan stayed in contact with Sean Faloon all the way through his six-month treatment.

A former priest who attended the centre at the same time has spoken of Finegan's refusal to 'actively and honestly' take part in group therapy sessions. Despite this, he was allowed to leave and return to his parish in the summer of 1995, without completing the full sex offenders programme. Local police were not made aware of the risk he posed, and instead Finegan was made to sign a contract giving his assurance that he would stay away from young boys.

Claire obtained a copy of this discharge contract, and it maddens me. The first lines read, 'My ongoing recovery is my priority. It is sustainable and life-giving. I will think positively about myself ...' And while there are clauses dealing with red flag issues, other parts upset me, such as, 'I will walk, play golf, listen to music, read good literature and [attend] theatre and concerts at least 4 times per month.'

Such carelessness, such inattention allowed him to go home like this.

Within two days of his return, he raped Sean Faloon in the parochial house.

The *Spotlight* crew had filmed me in the cemetery in Warrenpoint with Damian in order to demonstrate how difficult it had previously been to get to Mum and Brendan's grave without passing through the literal shadow of Finegan's Celtic cross. I remember there was snow falling while we filmed that day.

There were other sequences too, and I named him – which I was happy to do.

But at the eleventh hour, while the programme was being put together, my family let me know that they weren't happy. Things were happening quickly now, and my wife and children were worried about the effect it was having on me. And if this programme went out as envisaged, there'd be even more things happening. My family could see, absolutely, that it was right for me to name Finegan, but they wanted to know if I had to do it in full view or whether I could, as they'd seen people do in other documentaries, tell my story in silhouette. They also wondered if I could do it without some of the 'higher impact' things, such as standing by a cut-down grave on a snowy morning.

They were worried about what this was doing to me and, at the time, I thought they had a point. They were looking out for me. They weren't sure if I was strong enough for 'full exposure' just then.

I contacted the *Spotlight* team (probably to their disappointment) and asked if they could talk to me again, in the dark or the half-light. I went to Belfast, and we reshot the interviews; I talked to them instead from the shadows. In the clips where I was onscreen, they referred to me as Patrick.

The reason that I'm here where I am now, with this book – a book with my name and face on it, and little or nothing held back – is that I feel stronger now. Thanks to Roisin, my current counsellor, and the ongoing support of my family, I'm strong enough to do this. As Roisin put it, the little boy was maybe hiding again in the *Spotlight* programme. This book is my way of taking him from that hiding place by the hand. And the wee boy's name wasn't Patrick; it was Gerard.

I know from Claire and Kevin that a lot of other men have come forward as a result of the programme. And I take a quiet pride in that – the fact that it helped other people to come forward and seek their own justice. I also know of victims who haven't taken the legal route but have spoken to their own people, for the first time, about their abuse. Speaking in March 2018, Sinn Féin politician Conor Murphy, who had been a pupil at St Colman's four years after me and who had been physically, but not sexually, abused by Finegan, said that the Catholic Church, the school authorities and the wider education authorities all had questions to answer. 'They left him to abuse people without any interference [...] There was a system of administration in that school over a long number of years which allowed a paedophile to flourish [...] a man who was a violent, aggressive bully; a drunkard with an unhealthy interest in children.'

So 'Buried Secrets' did good work, but there's other work to be done; other questions to be answered. Why was Finegan allowed to retire, rather than be sacked? Why was he allowed to continue to exercise the greatest privilege of priesthood, to celebrate the Mass, after they knew who he was and what he'd done? How many other Finegans have there been?

How many are there now?

Chapter 22

LEAVING NEWCASTLE

'Buried Secrets' was broadcast on 14 February 2018. And around the same time I took my leave of my hometown, Newcastle. I knew the programme was going out – I wanted it to go out; I wanted to name Finegan – but I didn't want people in the town, who might recognise 'Patrick's' voice, coming across the street to put a hand on my shoulder and sympathise. I know it's something that would have come from a good place, but it wasn't something I wanted.

Although it was my hometown, it was a place in which I could be especially triggered. I could even be triggered by passing our old shop and home on Main Street – the place from which I'd been sent away to St Colman's College.

Newcastle was also the homeplace of Daniel Curran, another paedophile priest.

My parents and Daniel Curran's parents had been friends. They were lovely people, as far as I could tell. After the Brendan Smyth case, it came out that Curran had taken young fellas to a place the family owned in the beach area of Tyrella, plied them with drink and abused them. He was jailed in 2012 for four years, but after jail he came home … to Newcastle. I used to see him around the town, and it would take the ground from under me. On one occasion, in a local supermarket, I turned into an aisle and there he was at the far end. I abandoned my trolley where it was and just left – no, I didn't just leave, I *ran*. I ran until I got back to my own place, and I locked both doors leading into the flat, not feeling that he was a threat to me, but to the boy inside me.

That was the strength of the trigger.

Newcastle had also been the scene of the ultimate trigger: the last time I saw Finegan.

I was a young married man at the time, and the children were young. I had them about me, and we were walking up the Castlewellan Road towards the town, when I noticed a Mercedes at the pumps near St Patrick's Park. There was no one in it – they must have been paying for their petrol.

We were going past it, on the same side of the road, when Finegan came out of the shop. Of course I recognised him immediately, and I'm convinced that he recognised me in the exact same instant. I gathered the children across to the other side of the road immediately – so swiftly that they had no idea what was happening to them. I was with *my* children now and had an instinct to protect them. We absolutely had made eye contact, Finegan and me, which is why I'm so sure he knew me. There was no fear in him whatsoever. There never had been.

That encounter stayed with me for a long time. It's with me still.

Those were some of my reasons for leaving Newcastle, but where would I go?

My daughter Ursula lived in Poyntzpass and when a small house came up to rent, she thought it might suit me. It was close to her, her husband and the wee ones, and it was quiet; no one apart from them would know me and I just might find the peace I was looking for there. I went and had a look around and, lucky enough, I got it.

Poyntzpass is a tiny village. There's a filling station with a convenience store, a cafe and a couple of pubs. That's it, as far as 'commercial Poyntzpass' goes. But still it's very close to the A1, which would take you anywhere.

I hoped with all my heart that I'd find healing there.

Chapter 23

ARCHBISHOP EAMON MARTIN
AND UNFINISHED BUSINESS

In the months and years after the programme went out, I found myself still being annoyed by certain things. 'Buried Secrets' seemed to have led to a fresh stream of coverage about abuse, which flowed on without let. I would find myself nearly screaming at the newspapers and TV at some of the attitudes the Church was still taking. And I never believed it when it said, 'That was then; this is now.'

There was a sense of unfinished business for me, and it centred round a particular fact: on the floor of Newry cathedral there was a mosaic dedicated to Francis Gerard Brooks. As I've said, Brooks had also been a teacher in my time at St Colman's. He was the opposite of Finegan in some respects – spiky, stand-offish, severe – but that wasn't the point. The point was that the friendship that had existed between the two men was now known as a friendship that had protected Finegan, but not certain young boys. I wasn't the only one provoked by the fact that such a man had such a lavish memorial in a church. Some people who'd come forward after *Spotlight* were saying things like, 'I go to

Mass in Newry. What is Brooks doing on the floor of the cathedral?'

For the second time, I lifted the phone to make direct contact with the Catholic Church. I thought, 'If I'm going to speak to anyone, I'm going to the top.' And I phoned the office of Archbishop Eamon Martin, Primate of All Ireland since 2014; the most senior prelate in the country. I got the same woman who had visited me in the flat and turned up when I visited the school, and she said she'd make an appointment. She got back to me to say that a meeting had been arranged in the grounds of St Colman's itself, and I thought '*Really…?*'

We met instead in the Primate's residence, behind the cathedral in Armagh. I told Eamon Martin something of my story that day, but focused on the mosaic: how appalled I and other people were by such a tribute to someone so connected to Finegan and the cover-up around him. I received a call some days later, at the personal request of the Archbishop, and was told that it was going to be removed.

In a report in the *Irish News*, Eamon Martin was quoted as saying that he had met someone face-to-face who had brought things home to him … That was me. That the mosaic was going to be removed really helped. When the person rang me to give me the news, I'd cried. I cried because I'd been listened to – on that point at least.

But there were other points to be made, and I asked Eamon Martin's office if we could meet again. Our second meeting was in the parish centre opposite Newry cathedral where I'd met John McAreavey. At that meeting with Eamon Martin

I tried – as I'm trying in this book – to give life, if you like, to the word 'abuse', and all the damage it does. I'd seen and heard the word used a lot in the media, but often wondered about the understanding of it in people who hadn't suffered, including, maybe *especially*, people in the Catholic Church. My intention was to convey to him what 'abuse' entails, to tell him in graphic detail, so that when 'abuse cases' came across his desk again, he would appreciate the realities that exist within that term.

It was a difficult thing for me to do – to a man, to a stranger, to a senior person of the cloth. In the end, I filled up, and so did Archbishop Martin. It was, by no means, the end of everything, but when I came out on to the mall that day, I felt taller walking down the cobbles.

Chapter 24

A BIT OF PEACE

Redmond O'Hanlon GAC in Poyntzpass is the smallest GAA club in the county. Some of my grandchildren attend, and it is very close to where I now live. At the start, people at the club may have known who I was, but only in the sense that they knew my daughter and son-in-law, and that I'd sometimes be there to pick my grandchildren up. I was still keeping myself to myself – maybe a little too much.

My son-in-law began to invite me along to matches, and to watch when the kids were at training. My own love for Gaelic football had been arrested by Finegan taking me off the football field, and all through the glory years of Bryansford, Newcastle's local club, I'd never shown the kind of interest my friends had done. But, knowing I should get out of the house, I did what Ronan suggested. I dipped my toe in by going to the club when the youngsters were training. Often I'd be the only grandparent there, but I started to get so much fun out of seeing how much my grandchildren were enjoying themselves. The fun, and the sense of community, were so infectious. People had known me to see, but now they wanted to know my name. And as I became a more familiar face, people started coming over to me, people I didn't know: 'Aren't they doing well?' 'Isn't it great to see the young ones out training?' 'I remember when I was playing we used to rap doors to try to make a team ...'

Sometimes there'd be a hundred children out there in the different age groups. I wasn't actively taking part, but I started to look forward to the training. It was such a great way to knit myself into the life of a small village.

I found myself going to underage games all over Armagh. I didn't want to miss any, and the people were so welcoming. It lifted my spirits and improved my whole well-being. And I started doing wee jobs around the club as a way of thanking them – for accepting me into their community ... into their world. I hadn't spoken to anyone about my story, it wasn't something I felt I needed to do, but then it came up.

A charity walk was arranged along the tow path. It was a community event organised to raise money for the club and for cancer charities. While I was on the walk, I bumped into John McAreavey coming from the opposite direction. We didn't speak, but it affected me greatly.

The following day I was in company with Chairman Robert O'Neill and others from the club, when a reference was made to 'Bishop McAreavey' being seen on the towpath. 'Oh, he's not a bishop anymore,' someone said, 'after that case ...'

I don't know what showed on my face, but Robert asked if I was all right. I met him later and I don't know what it was about him, but I told him my story.

'I knew there was something,' he said, 'but I didn't know what.'

He was great with me. 'If you ever need to talk or go for a coffee,' he said, 'I'm here for you.'

I walk quite regularly now, usually with Eugene – a former captain and manager of Redmond O'Hanlon GAC – and two friends of his, who've become my friends too. Every Friday we go to the local cafe, and there's not a lot of sense talked.

These are my victories – the craic with them; the fun with the grandkids – and they are the only victories I really want. Along with the reclaiming of lost ground with Deirdre and my own kids.

I recently did some bits and pieces of painting around the club for a cross-community day we were hosting for Poyntzpass's most famous son, the rugby player Rory Best. I tidied up a few things and painted a silhouette of a young girl and fella playing Gaelic, jumping for a ball. It was nice to do a bit of art for something that was 'happy', and for the club that has done so much for me.

In the back of my mind, as I did the bits and pieces of painting, there had been *something* – something about being taken off a Gaelic pitch by Finegan. But on this pitch, on my own, I felt the arms of a community around me.

It felt like the opposite of abuse.

It felt like love.

POSTSCRIPT

In the early hours of 14 January 2022, I suffered a heart attack which I was fortunate to survive. Two months later, to the day, I had a life-saving quadruple bypass performed by Mr Alsir Ahmed and his team at the Royal Victoria Hospital, Belfast.

I know that there are many reasons why a person's heart might require such radical treatment, but I know, too, in my bones, that this is true: just as something can 'do your heart good', what Malachy Finegan and his friends in the Catholic Church did to me did my heart bad. It hurt my heart when I was young, and it did throughout my life until I was able to speak my own story; until I knew that it had been told.

I was so young, so very young, when I was abused by Fr Malachy Finegan. And that abuse took so much of my life. I don't think people understand how much an abuser takes away from you; how long a shadow they cast. I hope they might now. But my point, and the point of this book, is that an abuser needn't take *everything*. And that the shadow needn't follow you everywhere.

It's my experience that the Church had a huge say in how long my suffering lasted. In my case, they got it very wrong, year after year, which cost me time and peace of mind. It cost me *life*.

And what about now? Have they learned anything? Will it be better for the people taking cases about Finegan – and other Finegans – in the future?

At the end of September 2021, Archbishop Eamon Martin apologised for abuse carried out by priests in the Dromore diocese (priests like Finegan), and in his statement he said that the diocese was 'initiating a redress scheme for victims of sexual abuse', and 'reasonable compensation' was mentioned, with 'a cap of £80,000'.

My response to this, and to the whole of his statement was, 'Yes, *but* ...' Yes, because I *want* them to do something – I even want to *believe* them. I want to believe them when they say they have listened and learned, but I'm just not sure. I do know that anything they have learned they have learned at the expense of people like me. If there is any breach in their defensive walls, it is because of our very *breath*; because we attacked those walls with our shouting and pleading and imploring over the years. And to be honest, it was tiring.

But I have an appeal, one final appeal, for the Catholic Church: let go of your desire to seek to control the agenda. Don't say that there is a limit to compensation to people who are suffering endlessly. Come down off the altar, not with words, but with manifest humility. Tell us, in short, that you don't know what to do; that you're the last people who'd know what to do, having been the source of the problem.

And don't 'hold victims in your thoughts and prayers', not even at the heart of them, for that's still holding on. Hand the whole thing over. We are not your problems, we harbour your solutions. *And this, fundamentally, is not about you,* it is about us. Take off your armour, drop your hands to your sides, and surrender to that thought.

Is such a shift, such a transfer of power, remotely possible? I choose to believe that all or most things are.

I choose to believe that even now, somehow, in another dimension, the twelve-year-old me might be living another life: his own.

THANKS

From Gerard

There are so many good people woven into the fabric of
my story. I want to thank them all – I do thank them all
– but I can't thank them all here. There is not the room,
and I'd be frightened of forgetting a name. But I can't not
thank: the gang in Smarts' front room; everyone I met at
Nexus NI; everyone at Towards Healing in Dublin, and
my life-saving counsellors Hazel and Roisin; Doctors
McCleary, Devlin and Kelly, and Dr Martin Walsh; Sister
Theresa; Oliver King; all the staff and patients I did crafts
with at Finneston House; Yvonne M., for all the practical
help; my best friend, Micky, for always being there; all my
Celtic friends from Downpatrick and Glasgow; Claire
McKeegan, Kevin Winters and Ian Elliott; the *Spotlight*
team who worked on 'Buried Secrets'; the GAA family at
Redmond O'Hanlons; the Tow-Path Trackers; Suzanne
Breen, Neil Martin and Pat Lynch; Chris Moore, Claire,
Dr Rosie Burrows, Jon McCourt and Stephen Rea for
their endorsements; Kieran Griffiths and Chloe Harkin;

my sister-in-law, Bronwen Williams; Patsy Horton of Blackstaff Press for believing in this book, and Michelle Griffin for editing it; my brothers and my sister; everyone not named, but whose positivity built me up; my brother Damian – writer, confidant, and my guiding light through the darkness of putting this all together; Mr Alsir Ahmed, his team at the RVH Belfast, and all those who cared for me when my heart very nearly gave out; my beautiful family, and the best medicine I know, my grandchildren.

And finally I want to thank a twelve-year-old boy. A small boy I initially hated but grew to love.

From Damian

My thanks are all to Gerard, for his courage: his courage in the making of this book; his courage in taking a stand; the courage, and strength, of his vulnerability; and his courage in refusing to go back to St Colman's, which probably saved me from harm.

For I was maybe next in line.